Headhunter

Sheikhs, Japes and Questionable Deals

Matt Foster

Headhunter: Sheikhs, Japes and Questionable Deals

© 2025 Matt Foster

All rights reserved. No part of this book may be reproduced or transmitted in any form or by any means, electronic or mechanical, including photocopying, recording, or by any information storage and retrieval system, without prior written permission from the publisher. First edition, 2025.

Published by Vektor Publishing.

ISBN 978-1-83709-247-5

This is a work of non-fiction. Names, characters, businesses, places, events and incidents are used factually. Any resemblance to actual persons, living or dead, or actual events is purely coincidental. Printed in the United Kingdom.

For my children

"In the middle of difficulty lies opportunity."
— Albert Einstein

"All deals are questionable, until they pay off."
— Anonymous

"How the fuck did that happen?"
— Matt Foster

Prologue. Dubai 2017

I sat on the rooftop of my villa in Dubai, unmoving, staring into the night like a man already behind bars. The air was warm but heavy, and I barely noticed the breeze brushing across my skin. My eyes were fixed on the red and white barrier at the entrance to our private compound, blurred then clear, then blurred, then clear, as I blinked away the tears. I waited, for the inevitable burst of blue and red light to flood the adobe-covered guard hut and announce that it was over. That they had come. That everything I had built was gone.

Below and beyond me, the pool lay still and black, the water untouched since sunset. Just hours earlier, it had sparkled with laughter, my children's voices echoing off the stone walls as they splashed and played, safe and joyful. I had watched them from the poolside, with a cold beer and a warm heart. But now, under this silent sky, that pool looked like a grave. A grave for all my promises. For all the dreams I had dangled in front of my family, only to crush them with my mistakes.

Guilt gnawed at me like a physical pain. I had failed them, my children, my wife, everyone who had trusted me. The shame was almost unbearable. I felt like a fraud in my own home, a coward hiding in the shadows of everything he was about to lose.

Loneliness. Real, suffocating loneliness, not the kind cured by company but the kind that comes when you realise you have burned every bridge, and the only thing waiting for you is justice. Or vengeance. Or both. I was homesick too, strangely, though, I no longer knew what home meant. Not the house I had grown up in, not this villa bought with money that had come too fast and too easily. I missed a version of myself I could barely remember, a version that hadn't made such catastrophic choices.

I glanced down over the edge, catching the cold gleam of marble tiles three stories below, their smooth surface too unforgiving to ignore. A thought flared and thankfully died almost as soon as it came.

I looked down upon the patch of freshly dug earth in the garden, by the perimeter wall.

And I smiled as I recalled planting the bomb there.

I waited. Waited for the pounding fists on the door. For the sirens. For the click of handcuffs and the cold formality of being reduced to a number. I waited to be stripped of my possessions, my freedom, and the illusion that I was still in control. And when they were done taking all of that, I would be deported, sent back home to face the music I had composed with every lie I had told.

And still, the night held. Silent. Suspended. Cruel in its calm.

A red blush appeared in the distance.

Some peoples. 2003

I'm sitting in the office in Budapest one Sunny Thursday morning in mid-May. I know it was May because the outdoor swimming pools and lidos had just opened, marking the end of *we live in an industrial freezer where I can actually see the words coming out of my mouth* and the start of *if it gets any hotter I can't tell if I have yet to dry myself after the shower or I am already sweating.*

I was passing my time between getting up to go and flirt with Andika and being pulled into a meeting room to pass judgement on the latest aircon wars that had broken out between the Finance team and the IT practice.

My hobby during this period was registering domain names which would one day become invaluable and keep me in a salacious retirement. This particular morning, I had just bought MSSurface.de, in homage to the new Microsoft Surface touch screen gizmo.

My purple-and-pink-haired PA waddled over to my table. "Ello Mr Foster", with a big wide grin. "There is some peoples there to see you".

"Which peoples?" Half annoyed to be interrupted by the person I had hired to perform just such interruptions, partly peeved at the lack of the complete information I would require to decide whether or not to get up and put my jacket on, and mainly miffed as my own endeavours at private and personal enrichment had been put on hold.

"I think you need to come and see."

I frowned, puzzled, grabbed my jacket and rose to follow her to the boardroom. As I watched her leave, I remembered meeting her for the first time in the same boardroom. I had advertised for a data-inputter as we were planning a data-migration exercise. This bundle of energy and donuts bowled in before me, full of ready smiles and fake confidence. Vibrant neon hair and shiny shrapnel protruding from her nose.

If you cross over to the wrong side of the tracks, navigate a minefield, swim through shark-infested waters, and continue to cross to the wrong side of yet another set of tracks, you will arrive at where she was born and brought up. I immediately fell in love with her and offered her the challenge to be my assistant. 20 years later we are still firm friends, she still calls me Mr Foster, and it still sounds strange as I feel more like her proud dad.

She gets to the boardroom, turns to me with her hand on the doorknob, gives me a look which screams *I can't wait for you to tell me who the fuck these people are,* and she swings open the door.

I take a look at the 3 occupants of the newly painted room. It was a warm day, and the windows were flung wide open. The beige blinds clattering in the heated breeze. The wooden floors were starting to emanate that summer smell that exists in every country in the world apart from the UK, a velvety warmth and the almost imperceptible soupçon of sewage. You know, the smell you always remember after landing at your first Spanish airport. I was then and still am addicted to and captivated by it.

Three fucking massive giants.

Everything is relative of course. There was no actual beanstalk snaking its way through the polystyrene ceiling tiles, but this trio each stood approaching 2 meters tall, wide, bald, bedecked with gold chains, gold rings, gold teeth, and most likely, gold firearms. The overstretched leather jacket of the middle one squeaked like my nan's sofa as he lunged his right arm towards me.

"Meester Foster."

I let his fist eat my own like a Venus fly trap.

"Gentlemen, how can I help?"

Is how I remember the encounter now, sitting in my spacious oak-panelled office before a roaring fire in a well-to-do village in Northeast Derbyshire. In reality, I probably let out a high-pitched warble whilst managing to push out a sentence roughly related to "what do you want?"

Beer in the Square

"Well, what did they want?"

I was sitting in the leafy square next to the office, behind a cold pint of Dreher lager. Vicky, who 5 minutes previously had been told to get her coat and follow me, was stirring her Aperol Spritz vigorously, like an 8-year-old trying to rub out a rude word as the teacher approached.

I leaned forward, checked my surroundings as if I were about to tell a racist joke, cupped my hands on my chin. She leaned in. "Mafia." I said.

She stayed leaned in, and without saying "Er. . . Durr!" Gave me a look which said "Er. . . Durr!"

And then she said "Er. . . Durr!. . . No shit, Mr. Foster. What did they want!?"

I remember thinking at the time that although I had never benefited personally from a Hungarian secondary school education I was pretty sure that "No Shit" and "Er. . . Durr!" were not taught in English language lessons up and down the country, so I questioned whether she learned it from watching American sitcoms or from listening to me, strangely hoping that the slightest piece of Yorkshire DNA had been transmitted to this small part of Budapest and wondering how far and wide my vernacular seed would travel.

"What did they want!?"

I reached into my jacket breast pocket and slid out my wallet. Opening it, I withdrew the company debit card and pushed it across the table to Vik.

"Go get us another round in, I'll tell you when you come back."

She snatched at the card, bumping the chair back with her arse at the same time, rose purposefully, and strode briskly into the bar. I leaned back, exhaled, and thought about how I was going to start this thing.

Let me pause here for a second, because before I can tell you what happened next, I need to explain something.

You're a what?

You see, I'm a headhunter. And unless you've worked in certain corners of the corporate world, or had the misfortune of being phoned at 6:15 p.m. by someone asking if you're "open to new opportunities," you might not know what that actually means. So, let's start with the basics.

Most people, when they want a new job, go looking for one. They browse job boards, polish their CV, write a cover letter that uses the word "passionate" at least once, and send off applications into the void. That's one way to get hired.

But there's another side to the job market, a bit more hidden. That's where recruiters come in. Recruiters are people hired by companies to help them find employees. Instead of waiting for people to apply, recruiters go looking. They search through CV databases, online profiles, and their own professional networks, and try to match the right person to the right role.

Now, headhunters are a slightly superior breed. Where recruiters might fill a range of roles, including entry-level ones, headhunters are usually brought in to find someone very specific. Experienced. Qualified. Probably not looking for a new job. In other words, we chase people who aren't chasing us.

It's a bit like fishing, except instead of standing by a river with a rod, we're knee-deep in spreadsheets and LinkedIn profiles, trying to catch a particular fish who's already quite content in their current pond.

Our job is to convince them otherwise.

We contact them, politely, professionally, and with just the right amount of persistence, and we try to plant seeds. A little curiosity. A little doubt. Wouldn't it be nice to earn more money? To have a shorter commute? To work for a company that doesn't treat "pizza in the break room" as a motivational strategy?

If we do our job well, the candidate ends up seriously considering something they weren't even looking for in the first place. If we do it really well, they take the job, the client's happy, and we get paid. A lot.

So, in short, a headhunter is someone who finds people for jobs they didn't know they wanted and convinces them to take a closer look.

Right. Now that we've got that cleared up, let's take one more quick detour before we get back to the story.

You might be wondering how this whole business even came about. Recruitment agencies and headhunting didn't just appear out of thin air.

The idea of finding people to do jobs is, obviously, as old as work itself. But the recruitment agency as we know it really began to take shape in the aftermath of the Second World War. Soldiers were coming home, industries were rebuilding, and there was a massive demand for people to be placed quickly into all sorts of roles. Agencies started springing up to connect returning servicemen and women with available work.

In the decades that followed, especially during the economic boom of the 1950s and 60s, recruitment started to become a professionalised industry. Agencies moved from simply placing temp staff in admin jobs to helping companies find specialists, managers, and executives.

By the 1970s and 80s, executive search, or headhunting, began to grow in popularity. As businesses got bigger and more complex, they realised that finding the right leaders and senior professionals wasn't something they could leave to chance. It required expertise, discretion, and a bit of bullshit. Enter the headhunters.

Early headhunters often came from business backgrounds themselves. They knew the industries inside out, had networks full of useful contacts, and were not afraid to pick up the phone. They would cold-call candidates directly at their desks, with zero warning and even less apology. LinkedIn didn't exist. People had little black books. It was all very cloak and dagger.

Fast forward to today and the game has changed again. Technology has made it easier to find people but harder to get their attention. Everyone is more contactable, but also more cynical. There are algorithms, AI tools, psychometric tests, video interviews, and automated rejection emails that sound just human enough to sting. But at its core, recruitment, especially headhunting, is still about people persuading people.

And that's where I come in. One foot in the digital world, one foot in the old-school approach. A laptop in one hand, a phone in the other, and a well-rehearsed pitch in my head.

Alright. That's the background. Thanks for indulging me. Now, let's get back to the bit with Vik, the drinks, and the rather surprising turn this particular job took.

Swiss Roles

"Gentlemen, how can I help?"

My gaze bounced between the three men sitting opposite me, landing briefly on each one. One second per face. Just enough to look thoughtful, not enough to look desperate. It's a trick you pick up after years of presenting to multiple people.

Meanwhile, behind the calm exterior, my brain was going at full tilt. Who's in charge here? Who signs the cheques? Experience told me it was probably the one in the middle. He had the serene, slightly bored expression of a man used to getting his own way.

But what about the one on the left? Quiet. Arms folded. Face like a wet Monday in Moscow. Was he just bored, or was he the one I should actually be worried about? Sometimes the quiet one is the real power in the room. Sometimes they're just jet-lagged and trying not to fall asleep. You never know until they speak.

The one on the right looked like he'd wandered in by mistake. He was looking all around the room as if he was scouting for either a quick exit or a hidden camera, or probably both.

Then came the real question: What tone should I take? These were Russians. Russians do not do small talk. Russians do not want to know about my weekend, or what I'm watching on Netflix, they want numbers, timescales and bottom lines.

And most importantly, how much money could I wring from this situation? That was the game. Could I get them to pay more than they wanted, while still making them feel like they'd won? Could I walk out of here with a deal that paid for a large kitchen extension?

That was the challenge. Extracting as much cash as humanly possible from these inhuman giants in suits that probably cost more than my car.

And to do it with a smile. A calm, professional smile that said, *Trust me, I care about you not the fee*. Even though, that was of course, absolute bullshit.

The middle one spoke, tellingly without so much as a sideways glance at his companions. OK, it's him. Still, have to keep the others involved, influencers who are the real secret power brokers.

"Mr Foster, you are Headhunter, yes?" His voice was a thick Russian growl, like a bear that had just swallowed a gravel pit. It's always a strange moment hearing your own name pronounced for the very first time in a new accent. Oddly enough, in Hungarian, the word "Foster" apparently means either *Penis Square* or *Diarrhoea Square*, depending entirely on the tone. Hmm.

"We are indeed." I replied smoothly. "Executive Search Consultants." I nodded generously, sweeping my gaze across all three men to keep everyone feeling involved and important.

Then I paused. Another essential skill in the salesman's toolkit. Pausing creates a space for your prospect to chew-over what you've just said, which is even more important when dealing with non-native English speakers. It makes you look confident and, best of all, it stops you from accidentally giving away half your margin. I've seen too many recruiters ruin a deal because they couldn't resist filling every silence with another discount or extra perk. Sometimes the best move is to shut up and let the client say, "OK."

"Good. Good." He said, nodding slowly. "We have require of your services."

He stopped and looked at me. I nodded back, holding my silence. I could feel myself starting to take the lead in this little dance.

"We have acquired Swiss Roll factory."

At this point, I should remind you that everything you're about to read is true. One hundred percent God's honest. Well, mostly; The story begins some thirty years ago, so some of the dialogue has been lovingly recreated, like a wartime photograph that has been painstakingly colourised. I mention this so you understand that if I were making things up, would I invent such a ridiculous scenario as a Russian mafia mob having acquired a Swiss Roll factory?

You couldn't make it up. And I'm not.

Speaking of truth though, the Swiss roll is not Swiss. Let's get that out of the way.

Despite the alpine-sounding name, this elegant little spiral of sponge and jam most likely originated in 19th-century Austria or somewhere else that excelled in cake engineering. The Swiss themselves call it a Biskuitroulade, which sounds like something you'd get charged with at The Hague rather than eat with tea.

"A Swiss Roll factory?"
"A Swiss Roll factory."
"In Budapest?"
"Yes, in Budapest."
"Excellent. What do you need?"
"We need General Manager."
"It doesn't already have a General Manager?"
"It had. Accident."

I stared at the man in the middle. For quite a bit longer than is professionally advisable. I became aware that my mouth was hanging open and closed it quickly, nodding like this was all perfectly routine. As I reached for my legal pad and clicked my pen into readiness, I said, "Right. Let's go through some details."

At this point, it was best to fall back on the formal structure of taking a job brief. There were dozens of questions I wanted to ask, but I needed time. Time to steady my pulse, to regain control of both the meeting and my facial expressions. So, I avoided the more obvious follow-ups, such as "What kind of accident are we talking about?" or "Is the Swiss Roll factory haunted?" Instead, I took a breath, straightened my pad, and began the structured ritual of asking sensible recruitment questions while pretending everything was entirely normal.

Let us be briefed

Let's face it, asking a client for a proper job brief can sometimes feel like trying to pull teeth. You get vague job descriptions with phrases like "must be a self-starter," "dynamic team player," or "comfortable with change," which usually translates to *the fucking building is on fire and there's no time to train anyone*. But if you're going to find someone who actually wants the job and can do the job, you need the facts.

This is where you, the recruiter, become part detective, part therapist, and part negotiator. Grab your coffee, clear your diary, and let's dive in.

It starts innocently enough. You ask the client for "a quick 20-minute call to go through the role." They say, "It's all in the job spec." But you already know that document was last updated in 2017 and still references Windows 9. If the hiring manager isn't on the call, expect answers like, "I think it's a mix of admin and… something with code?" Always try to get the person the new hire will report to. That's where the gold is.

This is where you pretend not to already know the answers, so the client feels in control. Job title? Location? Is it remote, hybrid, or do they expect someone to teleport in daily? Ask about the salary range. If they say "competitive," you may translate that as "We don't want to say it out loud, but most of the current workforce have to nick coffee and bog roll."

Ask things like, "What does a typical day look like?" or "What would the new hire be doing most of the time?" One of the best questions is, "What kind of person wouldn't work out in this role?" That one always gets them talking. You're looking for the juicy bits: Real-world tasks, team dynamics, expectations, and any "oh by the way" surprises they forgot to put in the job description, like "must also run the company's TikTok."

The hiring manager may start reading from a 14-item list of skills. Politely stop them and say, "If I find someone with 9 out of 10, which one are you willing to drop?" They'll say "none." Smile. Ask again. Eventually, you'll find out that "experience with underwater basket weaving" is not, in fact, essential.

Ask about the team. Are they friendly? Chaotic? Brilliant but disorganized? Is the manager a hands-on mentor or more of a "Work it out for yourself and don't call me" type? You're trying to find out if this environment is more Google, more start-up chaos, or more "we hold meetings about meetings."

"How many interview stages?" you ask. "Just one or two," they say. Three weeks later, your candidate is preparing for Round Five with Dave from accounts who has heard your candidate has an impressive cleavage. Push for the real expected process: who's interviewing, what's involved, and how long they expect it to take. Then double it.

Now it's time for the most revealing question of all: "Why would someone want this job?" The manager blinks. Silence. Finally: "Well… it's a good team." (Always the first answer.) Push gently: Is there career growth? Cool tech? Free snacks? Flexible hours? No meetings on Fridays? You need something to sell beyond "we exist."

Before you finish, clarify how they want to work with you. CVs in batches or one at a time? Weekly updates or daily emails? Who signs off interviews and offers? This is where you lock in expectations, so no one forgets what was agreed.

Vik finished her drink and shook her head slowly.

"A Swiss roll factory?" she said.

"A fucking Swiss roll factory." I confirmed.

She blinked at me. "How the hell are we supposed to find a manager for a Swiss roll factory, owned by the mafia, when the last one had an 'accident'?"

"We're not." I said.

"You said no? To the fucking mafia?" Vik was staring at me like I'd just said no to the fucking mafia.

"I didn't say no. I said yes, but only if they pay $50,000."

"Matt, they might look dumb, but they're not. No way they're paying $50,000."

I gave her a look. "Catch up, Vik. I know they're not paying fifty. That's the point. I didn't say no. I just made it their idea."

"They said no?"

"They said they'd think about it."

She stood, threw back the rest of her wine like it was water, and gave me a look somewhere between admiration and exhaustion.

17

"Mr Foster, I swear, every damn day with you is an adventure. I've got to run." She leaned in and kissed me on both cheeks.

"Ciao. See you tomorrow," she said, already turning, heels clicking as she hustled toward the tram stop.

I sat back and watched her disappear into the thinning crowd. The square hummed around me, lazy and golden in the late sun. I caught the eye of a waitress and nodded at my empty lager glass. She smiled, a slow, knowing pout, then strutted off to the bar, hips swaying more than they actually needed to.

As I watched her go, with the sun beginning its descent behind the buildings, I started thinking. How did I end up here? Not just about how I ended up in Budapest, but how I ended up here. In this life. In this version of me.

The beginning

I was minted a headhunter on October 1, 1996. 27 years old and already on fourth career. The first being a Royal Air Force pilot, the second carrying the grand title of Assistant Customer Marketing Manager Carlsberg Tetley Southeast, the third, a publican.

I was actually offered the job during my first interview on Christmas Eve 1996.

A month before this, I was sitting in my office in Romford, Essex. The building used to be the Romford Brewery Company, before it was swallowed up by Carlsberg-Tetley. My role as Assistant Customer Marketing Manager Carlsberg Tetley Southeast gave me, apart from really wide business cards, plenty of time to peruse the newspapers whilst nursing a bottle of Carlsberg Ice and puffing on a Marlboro light whilst pretending to get some serious Assistant Customer Marketing Manager Carlsberg Tetley Southeast work done.

For some reason, the internal postman had put today's copy of the FT on my desk. Presumably because out of the team of the four of us in total, I was the only one with a degree, and also the only one who at 2pm was on his first bottle of Carlsberg Ice and not his 5th.

I flicked the pink sheets absently mindedly and hesitated when a job advert caught my attention.

Recruitment Consultant, Robert Walters PLC

I had experience of recruitment consultants, having been approached a few times in the past to consider amazing opportunities with rival breweries. My opinion of them wasn't the highest; a bunch of Jack and Jill the lads who spent the day cold calling enough people until they happened to alight on the one disgruntled employee whose boss had definitely given them a funny look that morning and got paid THIRTY-FIVE GRAND for doing it.

I think I must have given a cartoon double take.

£35,000? £35,000? Thirty-five fucking grand? That's what it said, plus car and commission.

I placed my bottle gently on the table and started to read the advert with a renewed commitment. No experience necessary, full training provided. It's got my name written all over this bad boy. My salary at the time was £18,702.

To apply, send your CV along with a letter stating your reasons for interest. I stubbed out my fag and turned to my computer, as one of my colleagues burped and another laughed as he knocked over his beer whilst pointing at the burper. Reasons? 1 reason. 35,000 reasons. Get me out of here.

Two weeks later, I find myself standing outside the offices of Robert Walters in Covent Garden. It's Christmas Eve, and twilight has just begun to settle over the city. The streets pulse with last-minute shoppers and merry revellers, some already half cut at half four, laughter echoing off the cobbles. The air is rich with the scent of roasting chestnuts and smoky hot dogs, a heady mix that blends perfectly with the warm glow spilling from the shopfronts dressed in festive lights.

Back up North, offices would be shuttered and the pubs overflowing by now. But here, in the capital's restless core, business doesn't wind down, it dips for the line. I glance across at a gaggle of city workers outside Porter's bar, their pint glasses raised in cheer, faces flushed with beer and cold.

For a second, a Sliding Doors moment: Behind me, the door to an interview, a possible future. Ahead, the easy way out, nerves drowned in ale and conversation, an anonymous night lost in the crowd. I tell myself I'll be back here in an hour. Maybe.

I turn, push the intercom and wait for the buzz. My buzz can wait.

An hour later, I'm riding the lift back down to the foyer, a grin plastered across my face, head spinning with possibilities.

The interview had started off a little shaky. The receptionist, who looked like she'd stepped off a Victoria's Secret runway, led me to what I'd later come to know and love as one of the fourth-floor interview rooms. She asked if I wanted something to drink. "Tea, coffee, DC?"

"DC? What's DC?" I asked. "Diet Coke," she replied, in the kind of tone you'd reserve for someone who just asked what year it is. Diet Coke? They give away Diet Coke here? For free? How much money was this place making? Judging by the sheer opulence of the offices and the number of wall-mounted TVs silently blaring out every news channel known to man, quite a fucking lot, thank you very much.

I say shaky start because after she brought me the tea I'd asked for and gently closed the door, I was left alone in that glassy box for much longer than expected. Twenty minutes past the hour, and still no sign of Jon, the guy I was supposed to meet. Was this some kind of test? These people are professional interviewers after all. Were they trying to psych me out? See how I perform under pressure?

I scanned the room for hidden cameras, half convinced there was a recruitment war room somewhere filled with more supermodels, analysing my every fidget in real time.

The door burst open and in flew a sharply dressed, pint-sized man with a wild mop of ginger hair. He hurtled toward me, thrusting out a hand mid-stride. "Matt, is it?" he beamed, slightly out of breath, voice thick with a Welsh lilt as we shook hands like old comrades. "Y—" I began. "I'm Jon. Sit back down." He said, motioning to the chair I'd just vacated. He dragged out one for himself and collapsed into it, legs stretched casually in front of him.

I took a second to clock him properly. Despite the chaos of his hair, the rest of him was razor-sharp. His initials were stitched into the cuffs of a spotless white shirt. A silver Rolex winked from under the sleeve of a perfectly-tailored navy suit. His shoes, parked neatly beside mine, gleamed like mirrors.

He didn't skip a beat. "Matt, it's Christmas Eve. It's half past five. I've got two more bloody meetings after this." He slapped a briefcase onto the desk, pulled out a legal pad and pen, and kept going. "Every other bastard in the city is already half pissed. By the time I make it to the pub, it'll be the same time I usually get home, which means by the time I do get home the dinner will be in the dog and I won't get a shag."

He clicked the pen with a snap and flipped open his notepad. "So, tell me. Why the fuck would you want to be a recruiter?"

The end

I absolutely loved him.

I floated out of the office into the throng of Covent Garden at roughly 7pm. The air was crisp and forged a piercing motorway through the nasal passage directly to the brain. Roast chestnuts, Christmas lights, smart suits, crowded pub doorways. Jon had offered me the job there and then, and I had quickly and happily accepted. I was coming to London baby!

Christmas day saw me and my girlfriend, my mum and dad, brother, aunts, uncle and grandmas back at the family pile in Yorkshire. I took the rare opportunity to spend some one-on-one time with my dad.

He was a big man, both in stature, and in the presence he emanated. It's true to say our family was a patriarchy, and whilst we didn't see my dad as often as we liked; He was a senior executive in the brewing industry, he remained the lynchpin of the Foster clan.

He was my idol, both in business and in life. We would rarely disagree, never argued. The last time I could remember any hint of discord was when a spoiled sassy 18-year-old me, for reasons I honestly cannot remember, spurted out "I can't wait to leave here and go to university". He didn't rise to it, he didn't even look disappointed as the old trope goes. He just looked a little emptier than before my bratty outburst.

It's an exaggeration to say he lived for his sons; His career, my mum and his mum all received a healthy fair share of his attentions, but he relished being a dad and he was excellent at it. As I am writing this my thirteen-year-old is telling me she would rather chop wood with me today for the Christmas fire, than go to school and do triple maths. I just looked her in the eye and told her to hang her uniform neatly and get her wellies on. Dad would have done that.

It was that limbo hour on Christmas day afternoon, the frivolities of lunch having passed, yet still too early for the local to throw open its doors. My dad's study sported a marvellous pair of green leather Chesterfield armchairs, we had each chosen one and poured ourselves into its warm embrace. He had lit us both a substantial cigar and we were savouring a bucket of Port each, the size of which would have immobilised a pair of less accomplished drinkers.

As a senior figure in the brewing world, my dad often found himself the target of headhunters' persistent affections, constantly being courted by recruiters eager to snatch him away for new opportunities. Because of this, his residual opinion of my new chosen profession was never overly favourable, as he saw us as opportunists always trying to pull people into roles without fully understanding the nuances or the realities behind the jobs. Yet, despite this scepticism, he never cast too harsh a judgment on my own career choice. Instead, he offered a measured piece of advice, one that was simple but carried a weight of experience: "If you are going to do it, really do it. You don't have to be perfect, just better than everyone else."

Those exact words have stayed with me ever since, and I have shamelessly plagiarized that phrase more times than I can count. Over the years, I have passed it on to the next generation of recruiters, from the Baltic states to the Balkans, as a kind of guiding mantra, a reminder to strive not for perfection but for excellence and distinction in an often-unforgiving industry.

Boxing day was an equally gluttonous affair. After a lunch lacking only flagons of meade and a roasted swan, my girlfriend and I jumped into my Carlsberg company car to start the journey back to our house in Essex.

It was an uneventful journey down the A1. My mind was full, swirling with a mixture of emotions. Memories of the perfect family moments we had just shared played over and over in my head, warm and vivid, like a film on repeat. At the same time, I found myself silently rehearsing the resignation speech I planned to deliver to my boss at Carlsberg. The words felt heavy yet thrilling, this was the turning point I had been waiting for, the moment I would finally step into something bigger.

We stopped along the way for petrol, cigarettes, and a bottle of wine that my girlfriend had decided would be her snuggle blanket for the rest of the journey back to the smoke. I watched her settle in, clutching and drawing from the bottle warding off the creeping chill of the December night. As I restarted the engine of the Audi A4, the familiar hum of the car filled the air. I remember thinking how much I would miss it, the sleek lines, the smooth power, and especially the carphone, which perfectly suited the lofty status of an Assistant Customer Marketing Manager Carlsberg Tetley Southeast. Yet even as I acknowledged those comforts, I reminded myself that the doubling in salary waiting just around the corner would more than make up for leaving it all behind. Life was good, no, life was great. But at 26 years old, with a lucrative job on the horizon, it was about to be something else entirely, fucking perfect.

Suddenly, the carphone blinked, flashing green. An answerphone message. Who the fuck was working on Boxing Day? The thought caught me off guard. With a curious but slightly irritated frown, I pressed the buttons to retrieve the voicemail, wondering what could possibly interrupt this perfect night.

It sounded a bit like my mum, but more desolate, and crying.

"Matthew. It's mum." Long pause. "Come back home." Emptiness. "Your dad's dead."

Life on pause

My Dad's dad passed away at the age of 53. Lol. (No, not like that, he was christened *Laurence*, this is a sad bit). I was one year old at the time, so most if not all of my memories come from stories. Actually, did you know that's it's a fact that when we remember an event, we are not actually remembering the event, we are remembering the LAST TIME WE REMEMBERED that event. True that, look it up.

Grandad Foster was a coal miner by trade, a horny-handed man of the earth who spent his life beneath the soil. For thirty-five long years, he rose before daylight, stepping out into the cold, black morning to make his way to the pit. He spent his working hours in the half-light of the tunnels, crouched and sweating in the dust, swinging tools and shifting rock. When his shift ended, he came home late, shoulders slumped, blackened skin scrubbed raw at the kitchen sink, lungs aching from the air he had no choice but to breathe. That rhythm shaped his life, and through it all, he earned a sense of dignity, a steady living, and a family who loved him for the man he was.

It also earned him something else: Black Lung Disease, known by the doctors as pneumoconiosis. Years of inhaling coal dust carved deep into his lungs and slowly pulled the breath from his body. In time, it took him, as it had taken so many of his kind. His candle went out quietly. If I am being honest, mercifully for me and mine, not before he had done the most important thing a man can do. He had brought Dennis into the world, his only son, my father.

My dad also only lived to see his fifty-third birthday. As I sit here and write these words, my own fifty-fourth birthday is just around the corner. So, you will forgive me if I type a little quicker than usual. There is something unsettling about knowing you have now lived longer than your father did. It makes your fingers move faster, as if trying to outrun something that has already begun to catch up.

The Reaper's choice of exit ticket for my dad, as we learned later, was Ischemic Heart Disease. A rather clinical name for what was essentially a long, silent throttling from the inside. The sort of thing that creeps up wearing a white coat and a clipboard, not a cloak and a scythe. Growing up the son of a miner in the 1950s, my dad enjoyed what the doctors call nowadays a "high-risk lifestyle" and what they called themadays "tea." His diet was nothing if not varied, assuming your definition of variety includes multiple forms of fat and the occasional potato. There was fat spread generously on bread, fat bubbling away in the chip pan, and fat infused into every lovingly scorched slice of meat fried beyond recognition.

The only thing green in the kitchen was the mould if you forgot to clear the fridge. Butter was applied with a coal shovel, salt came in by the sack, and any meat that wasn't at least 40% gristle was viewed with suspicion. He didn't drink to excess, didn't smoke much, and still, Death took one look at his coronary arteries and said, "That'll do."

There was no dramatic finale. No collapse at the wheel or clutching at the chest during a family barbecue. Just a gradual narrowing of the roads inside him until, on that Boxing day, as his youngest was navigating the A1 towards the life his father had set him up for, alone in his favourite chair, his traffic stopped. It's no surprise, when your childhood diet is basically a dare, the bill eventually comes due.

I didn't get to use my well-rehearsed resignation speech, but resigned all the same, quietly and tearfully, the next day over the phone. We had turned the car around and sped back up the motorway, the howling of the engine drowning out that of me. I didn't take the headhunter job. Instead, along with my brother, who also resigned, I moved back to Yorkshire to live with and prop up my mum.

Being from the industry, we bought a pub. Years later when decorating a house built in the Middle Ages, I researched the Foster family tree in order to decorate a kitchen wall. The main motif of the family coat of Arms consisting of 3 drinking cups representing my dad, my brother and me, I like to think.

An accomplished recruiter is like a dog with a bone, relentless and single-minded, sniffing at the arse of every potential target, and over the course of the next 9 months, I received call after call from Jon from Robert Walters, telling me should I ever tire of throwing drunken women out of a grade 1 listed building after catching them adorning the bathroom walls with the fruit of their own tampons, at midnight, in the rain, in advance of pulling an all-night VAT return ordeal, then his offer most definitely stood.

I held out until October.

I spoke with my brother. There was no denying that the business would greatly benefit from the quarterly commissions I would be able to inject into its anaemic cash flow. And whilst my mum was far from back on her feet, she was thankfully off her knees. I was to pack my car, and like millions before me, head south to the Smoke to seek my fortune.

You know the silly things you miss when they aren't readily available? For instance, one time in Budapest our local Tesco, yep, there is, managed to source a pallet of Heinz baked beans. My scarcity mindset took over, and I loaded up the boot of the Maserati. Years later, as we were packing to leave for Dubai, I half-filled a wheelie bin with the self-same tins of beans. I can't stand baked beans. Never have.

They were never really British to begin with you know.

It all kicked off in 1337, when King Edward III of England decided he quite fancied being King of France as well. Possibly because of the wine, possibly the climate, but most likely, historians agree, because of the topless beaches. The French, predictably unimpressed, responded with a firm "Fuckez-Vous Off" and so began what we now call the Hundred Years' War.

While English troops survived long sieges on a diet of stale bread, beer, and Kendal mint cake, the French were dining on something far heartier: Cassoulet. A bubbling, meaty bean stew, calorie-laden and morale-boosting, it varied depending on which part of France your moustache was from. Toulouse favoured duck and Carcassonne added lamb.

After 116 years, the English were eventually pushed from Bordeaux to Calais, and finally back across the Channel. We may have lost the war, but we gained something arguably better. A recipe. At the cost of the deaths of many English spies, one finally managed to return with notes on the magical bean stew that had fuelled the French war machine and thus began Britain's long love affair with the legume.

Fast-forward to 1895. Enter Henry J. Heinz, who looked at cassoulet and thought, "What this needs is a fuckload of sugar and putting into a tin can. Sales didn't take off right away, in fact orders were initially incredibly poor, but 5 years later, somebody invented the tin opener, and the product began to soar. By 1901, Heinz Baked Beans had made their voyage back across the Atlantic, and in 1928, a factory in Harlesden was established.

But what of beans on toast? That peculiar British masterpiece?

1940. Hitler, having flattened most of Europe, sets his sights on Britain. Operation Sea Lion is hatched, a full-scale invasion by sea and air. Churchill, ever the strategist, heads to the Kent coast to observe.

To pass the time, Churchill and his cabinet settle in for a long game of cards in a windswept bunker. At some point, refusing to leave the table, he barks for sustenance. An aide obliges, layering his beloved Heinz beans between two slices of toast. And just like that, a national dish is born.

London baby!

Here are the things a Northerner, or rather this Northerner, or more particularly this Barnsley Tyke, missed whilst living in London. In no particular order.

A head on a pint of beer, driving to a supermarket, driving anywhere. Fish and chips, having a garden, owning a pet, wearing wellies, and being a regular in a local. Some of these you begin to notice almost immediately, others grow on you over a period of time and only become noticeable once you break through the tractor beam of the M25.

Those first few days and weeks in our Capital though offered nothing but positive experiences. Day 3 as a headhunter, Wednesday evening. After a few beers with my new colleagues in Browns, Covent Garden, I arrive back at the hotel which would be my London pad for the first 4 weeks. I insert the key card into the door, enter the spacious suite, and throw my briefcase onto the bed. Just as I am wondering whether to start my retirement ritual, or to pop out to the pub across the road for a couple more nightcaps, my phone buzzes in my suit pocket.

It's Jon, my boss of the last 72 hours.

"Fozzy! 'ow are you? 'ow's the 'otel?"

Sorry, I should have warned you to read that part in the voice of an overenthusiastic Welsh commercial radio DJ. Let's try it again.

"Fozzy! 'ow are yoo? 'ow's the 'otel?"

I really liked Jon. A diminutive yet stocky Welshman from the valleys. He carried himself with the flamboyance of a Victorian necromancer. I could imagine him at the other end of the line, swirling a cape around his face and stamping his cane firmly on the floor as he erupted the question.

"I'm good, It's good."

"Good, good, very good. 'Ave you got a pinstripe suit?"

I looked at myself in the mirror. My suit, the only one I owned, was green, and not a little shiny. My hair was shorter than I usually carried it, due to having my blonde highlights cut out a few days before joining. And the hole in my ear which until recently had sported a diamond earring was healing over nicely. No, I did not own a pinstripe suit. I told him so.

"Right, listen, before you come in tomorrow, get to Gieves and Hawkes, get a grey chalkstripe double breasted on my account."

"OK, cool. How come?"

"Eh, oh, we have a big client meeting tomorrow, you and me"

Client meeting? Why would the Divisional Director be taking the newest of his 50 or so employees to a client meeting? My first 3 days had consisted solely of classroom-based theoretical training, and whilst I was taking to it like the proverbial duck, I was quite sure that the time was not yet upon us when I should be unleashed upon an unsuspecting public.

So I'm savouring the feeling of the newly acquired woollen suit on my thighs, as Jon and I wove through The Mall traffic in our black cab. A sunny yet bitingly frigid October mid-afternoon. My dad's old briefcase snuggled on my lap for comfort and succour. Within, the new pen and notepad my mum had bought me for such just occasions, I felt like an 11-year-old again in his first week at big school. Jon had sensed my nervousness and was doing his best to keep the proceedings matter of fact and light-hearted. He was actually doing a good job of it. This was one of Jon's great management skills; take the work seriously, but yourself not too much so.

Saint James Park glided (glid?) greenfully past on our left. To our right, St James Palace, which had, in 1809, rather conveniently partially burned down thus allowing George III to claim on the insurance, vastly overstating the number of CDs he had lost in the process, and move his family into the 775 roomed building which was looming ever larger though our windscreen.

We entered the roundabout and slowed to a crawl approaching a majestic looking set of black and gold open gates. Jon was shuffling forwards in his seat, reaching for his wallet, and leaning forward to the driver. We slowed even further. I looked around. Tourists bimbled around the fence, the gates, the car. We stopped to let a gaggle of Japanese schoolgirls centipede their way across our path, then slowly edged forward again, through the open gates. Not past the open gates, through the open gates. I looked at Jon, he caught me in his peripheral, barely able supress a grin as he fixed his gaze on the driver who was counting his change.

"Yep." He smirked. Still pointedly avoiding eye contact with me.

The cab crunched to a halt. A besuited middle-aged gentleman in a morning suit, who I remember thinking at the time looked strikingly like Roger De Courcey, took a hold of the cab's handle and opened the door to my left.

I looked at him, and past him, to the august building behind. My first ever meeting as a headhunter, after 3 days behind the wheel was to be here, inside the Queen's gaff, Buckingham Fuckingham Palace!

I can't remember the exact details of the next hour or so, that was after all nearly 30 years or more than 20,000 pints ago. I do remember the meeting was with a senior aide of Prince Charles. The Duchy of Cornwall was in need of a new Finance Director - I didn't ask what had happened to the old one, this was only 3 months after Diana so I kept my mouth shut - And we were going to be the firm who would find his successor. I do recall though I put up a surprisingly good account of myself though and that if I had entered the meeting as a nervous caterpillar, I was leaving as a butterfly.

This was the skill, nay, the genius of Jon. He saw within me the potential and engineered a situation to unzip it. He could have taken any number of his 50 staff to that meeting that day. A more experienced one, a more attractive one, one more charming, one frankly less Northern, yet his actions that day were for the long-term benefit of both me and the firm, even with the potential short-term sacrifice of losing an assignment. He pushed me off a cliff and forced me to build my wings on the way down. I did, and I flew.

My life has been shaped by a handful of such lessons doled out by talented visionaries such as Jon, my dad and as I still remember, one of my Air Force flying instructors.

It was a hot summers' day in Shropshire in the early 90s. Made all the more stifling by the glass cockpit canopy of my Bulldog T1 aircraft. I was about 5000 feet in the air, seated to the left of said instructor. Even with the tinted visor down, here above the Staffordshire clouds, the piercing rays of the sun tickled tears from your eyes.

Apart from the visceral rush involved in a take-off, or the *holy fuck if I get this wrong, we are worm food* feelings that accompany every landing, the actual flying of an aircraft can be quite boring. Even in the tightest cerebral straitjacket my mind would find a way to wander.

In a small trainer aeroplane ('It's not a plane, Foster a plane is a vast expanse of land!'), devoid of radar, an important part of the task at hand for the driver is a constant and regular lookout. This involves casting your eyes to your left wingtip, scanning the horizon for aircraft, before rolling your head backwards, upwards, and to the right to scour the sky above through the glass canopy, with your vision coming to rest over the right wingtip. When not involved in any other important aspects of piloting, such as practicing a stall turn or peeing into a rubber tube, this practice should be enacted roughly every 30 seconds. Or in my case, whenever the instructor, infuriated with your forgetting what you should be up to, would scream "lookout!" into his mic and through your earpiece.

So we are bimbling along in a sweaty cloudless paradise when my earpiece crackles.

"Foster, I think we have an issue with comms, just going to unplug you for a second."

He reached forward to the left and unplugged the 3.5mm jack plug which fed from my helmet into the cockpit dash, cutting off all audio, from the tower, from other aircraft and from my instructor. Devoid of the whistling static I continued on our journey, in this case we were tracing the path of the M6 far below back home to base.

A couple of minutes later, a click in my ear and the return of the fizzling pops.

Another minute.

"Lookout"

Oh yeah, shit.

Left wingtip, clear, canopy, clear, right wingtip, FUCKING HELL!

A second Bulldog, flying straight and level to my right. Her left wingtip no more than 20 feet from my right. The pilot, a much more gifted driver than I was, grinning at me beneath his half-face visor, his white leather glove propped up with the middle finger, like an offensive circus tent.

"I have control." Barked the instructor.

I settled back onto my parachute, my joystick jerked violently to the left and forward as he put the aircraft into a steep descent, the nose pointed back toward base and the distant shoelace which formed the runway. Beside it, the crew room, where a few minutes hence I would be standing in front of the CO's desk and enjoying a one-way conversation without coffee.

It was a harsh and effective—OK, arguably sociopathic and potentially suicidal—lesson, but as lessons go, it affected me more deeply and permanently than memorizing the names of Henry VIII's unfortunate wives. It also taught me that effective management, whether of fighter pilots, headhunters, or any other profession, should include drama and exaggeration. Go big or go home, I thought as I sat there feeling small while he flew us home.

Trivia nugget: I was in the same squadron as one Jed Mercurio, whom I used to call 'Beany'. The RAF is full of hilarious such nicknames. Our instructors were 'Creamies' owing to them being such good pilots that they were 'creamed' off the top to train us not so gifted aviators. The desk-based officers were known as 'Shinies' on account of the shine on their trouser seat given its almost constant contact with a chair. I called him Beany, on account of the fact that he looked like Mr Bean. Yeah, Beany, you may have written such blockbusters as Line of Duty and Medics, but I got a book published which contains the phrase 'Buckingham Fuckingham Palace' so I reckon that's at least one all.

Black card

Those first couple of years at Robert Walters were thoroughly enjoyable. I was taught the art of, and did rather well in, recruiting newly qualified accountants away from the audit giants and placing them into controlling roles within more traditional commerce and industry type companies.

My mentor at the time was a thoroughly likeable and utterly posh young Fulham lad, who I'll call Rufus. A year younger than me but somehow boasting a couple more years of recruiting experience, he worked the same market as I did. Jon, displaying his usual wisdom, paired us up for mutual benefit. Occasionally, OK, quite often, fine, every single day after work, we'd dive across the road into Porter's bar to wash away the stresses and strains of city recruitment and share the latest hints and hacks about one of our darkest arts, 'Name Gathering.'

The year was 1997, and as mentioned earlier, six years before LinkedIn, the recruiter's weapon of choice, was even dreamed of. Back then, before you could approach an unsuspecting qualified accountant with a juicy new role, the first challenge was finding out who they actually were. Every recruiter had their favourite way of mining for gold, the names of our soon-to-be sold candidates.

Some would pretend to represent a new-to-the-market accountancy magazine and sweet-talk the receptionist into handing over a list of newly qualified accountants to send free copies to. Others would call the switchboard and ask for "Rob Jones." The inevitable reply was, "Rob who?" The perfect comeback was, "Rob Jones, he audits in the publishing industry." A win would be the receptionist triumphantly announcing, "Actually, the person specialising in publishing is Amanda Smith!"

Thanks.

One of my favourite tricks was bribing our fragrant team assistant to call the company switchboard with a story about meeting a charming young Lothario in a bar the night before who happened to be a successful accountant in the transport sector but, alas, she couldn't remember his name. It rarely failed.

One biting night during the Christmas season, Rufus and I stumbled out of Porters, feeling considerably worse for wear, and proceeded toward the tube station along the Strand. Our path led us past the headquarters of Price Waterhouse, a colossus in the accounting industry.

Rufus paused by the sliding double doors of the building's impressively vast entrance hall. In his unmistakably aristocratic Enid Blyton accent, he inquired, "Fozzy, are you inclined toward some merriment?"

"What like?"

He gestured through the glass walls to a rather magnificent Christmas tree, approximately thirty feet tall, gracing the foyer. "Do you think you could fall into that?"

I followed his gaze. It appeared enormous, adorned with spiky branches, a fair amount of glass ornaments and electric lights.

"Absofuckinglutely!"

As I said, we had sunk a few.

My next memory was of flailing and sprawling across a small section of that once-vertical Christmas tree. A bewildered and not entirely amused security guard hauling me to my feet, a concerned receptionist hurrying towards me, and Rufus making a discreet retreat back through the door we had just entered, a noticeable bulge protruding from beneath his large cashmere overcoat.

We met back out on the street, and he quickly moved ahead, motioning for me to follow closely behind. Once we had put a good distance between ourselves and the building, he slipped quietly into a side street, looking around to make sure no one was watching. Then, with a slight flourish, he pulled from beneath his coat an old-fashioned paper phone directory.

This wasn't just any old directory. It contained the names, job titles, and direct telephone numbers of the roughly 4,000 people working in the building. Up until a few minutes earlier, this invaluable information had been sitting right behind the now empty reception desk, completely unattended and easy to access.

It's spring, and Rufus and I are in the office. Technically. At least our jackets are, draped over the backs of our chairs. The thing about our Covent Garden HQ, given the growing scale of our business, was that it spanned four floors. Meeting rooms where we spent half our lives grilling aspiring FDs and CFOs were on the top floor. The trading floor was on the first. So if someone wasn't at their desk, they were either upstairs conducting interviews or, in our case, across the road playing pool.

Rufus was bent over the table, trying to win back the tenner he'd just lost to me, by sinking a tricky black, when his phone rang. He slid off the table, pulled his Motorola from his back pocket, and flipped it open like a cowboy with a revolver.

"It's Rufus."

I leaned on my cue and watched him pace, nodding along, distracted enough that I briefly considered nudging the black closer to the cushion. Then he snapped the phone shut and turned to me, grinning.

"C'mon, Fozzy. Grab your gear. New client in Ealing."

Twenty or so minutes later we were in the back of a black cab, bouncing through Notting Hill. Jen, our team secretary, had taken the call and passed it on.

"A chicken shop?" I asked, eyebrows raised.

"Apparently." Rufus said with a shrug and a smirk.

"A chicken shop. Not KFC. Just a chicken shop. Why does it need a Finance Director?"

"Well, not just one shop apparently. They've got half a dozen. And the best part" he checked his Tag Heuer "it's 3pm, ten minutes from mine. In, out, and we're done. Early bath or pub."

An hour later we were in the King's Arms in Fulham. Two pints, two jackets, and two buckets of free chicken courtesy of Robbie, the South African owner who had just spent an hour charming our socks off.

"You thinking about it?" I asked as Rufus lined up a shot.

He straightened. "Three years at Walters, Fozzy. That's a full term in most languages. What next? Page? Hays? It's all the same stuff."

He missed an easy stripe, stood back and raised an eyebrow. "What do you think?"

"He seemed sharp. Big plans." I gestured to the shelf. "And free chicken. Plus, a hundred grand."

"There's that." Rufus said, grinning.

Robbie turned out to be far savvier than we'd given him credit for. His ten-store chicken empire was just the start. He had plans, big ones. New outlets, a central HQ, overseas expansion, and VCs ready to throw in cash. And rather than hiring through us, Robbie had made the obvious move: Offer Rufus a desk, a hundred grand, and tell him to do it all from the inside. It was cheeky, especially given the fact I was sitting right next to my friend at the time, but bold, and it made commercial sense.

Fulham's a small village. Robbie and Rufus had enough mutual friends that when Robbie started asking around for a good recruiter, more than a few pointed him straight in Rufus's direction. By the time we walked into that meeting, the deal was already halfway done.

He took the offer.

Over time he worked his way up, sideways, sometimes backwards, then back up again. Now, as I write this, he is the Group CEO of a very well-known global chain of chicken restaurants, thankful every day, I am sure, that he said yes to that cheeky offer 25 years ago.

Still waiting for my black card, mate.

Moving on up

People often ask me, "What one piece of advice would you give to someone starting a career in recruitment?" Actually, no one's ever asked me that. Not once. But if they did, my answer would be the same as the advice I'd give the Mayor of Venice: don't burn your bridges. Allow me to explain.

After Rufus left, things at Walters just didn't feel the same. It wasn't long before I took the chance to spread my own wings.

As it happened, the opportunity came through another South African. Rather oddly, a senior figure at the company I was working for at the time.

At the time, our organisation was going through a major financial "event," as they call it. For a private company, an event could mean an IPO; A stock exchange listing, a private sale to a competitor, a management buyout (MBO), or even a BIMBO - yes, really - where management and a few friends buy the company. These kinds of projects always require extra strength and depth in the finance and legal teams for the duration.

That extra strength showed up in the form of Burt, a well-known financial genius and corporate shitkicker.

Normally, our paths wouldn't have crossed much; Him at the top of the corporate ladder, me one of the many holding it steady at the bottom. But since we were both smokers, we became firm friends after many chance meetings in the smoking room. That's right, what your company now calls the Yoga, Breakout, Zen, or whatever fucking Kumbaya studio, used to be a space dedicated solely to the pursuit of filling your lungs with delicious, deadly fumes.

Burt was a slight South African of Jewish heritage, with a wild explosion of jet-black hair that made him look like a young, rogue scientist. His thick, black-rimmed glasses demanded a nose substantial enough to support them, and nature had obliged. We bonded over a shared love of the absurd. He was a brilliant pessimist, and I always looked forward to our exchanges.

One late autumn afternoon, I got an email from Burt. It simply read, "Matt, pop up." I assumed he meant for me to visit him in his office on the fourth floor, rather than leap out from behind a sofa, so I grabbed my jacket and headed to the lift.

Out of habit, I turned right when I stepped out, towards the interview suites where I usually worked, before remembering I was here to see Burt. I had never turned left out of those lifts before. That direction led to the C-suite, home to the CEO, COO, CFO, and of course, Burt.

I pivoted and headed the other way. Outside the door marked "Burt LaSalle," I knocked and eased it open.

"Come in!" came the familiar voice.

I stepped inside and was immediately struck by the sheer size of his office. It was as big as the entire space my twelve-person team shared downstairs. I couldn't help but wonder: why do senior execs need so much room? Do they do laps after every deal? And why did he have three desks?

I approached the middle one, clearly his command post, and shook his hand before settling into a leather swivel chair that looked like it belonged on the bridge of a villain's spaceship.

"I want to pick your brains." He said, leaning back.

For the next 20 minutes, Burt told me a story. As a professional contractor, he kept a close network of top-tier headhunters so that one contract could roll into the next. One of those firms, based just streets away, was run by a man named Simion Katz, well-known in finance circles and, like Burt, a proud member of the Mill Hill Massive.

The firm was called SKA, presumably short for Simion Katz Associates, as opposed to any kind of homage to the music genre that originated in Jamaica in the late 1950s, and which was to be the precursor to both rocksteady and reggae.

SKA had built its reputation placing senior finance contractors and had been doing so since the late 1960s. Until recently, they had never touched the permanent market. But that was about to change.

For whatever reason, Simion had decided the time was right to expand into permanent placements, specifically for senior finance roles, FDs and CFOs. Burt, it turned out, had already mentioned my name.

I say, "for whatever reason," but the truth is there were plenty of good reasons. This was the late 1990s, the height of the dot-com boom. Cheap capital, speculative investment, and the rise of the World Wide Web had led to a gold rush of startups run by fresh-faced computer science grads. They could build a last-minute holiday website in their sleep, but running a company? Not so much. Most couldn't run a fucking bath.

That's where the grey-haired CFOs came in, professionals who could steady the ship, navigate compliance, and keep these adolescent CEOs out of trouble. Demand for permanent senior finance talent was exploding, and Simion Katz had correctly seen an opportunity.

Now, he just needed someone to build that division.

I chose a different bar that evening, the lobby of Brown's Hotel in Mayfair. Dressed as a lone businessman in an expensive woollen pinstripe suit, I would blend in seamlessly with the others. I didn't want any interruptions; I needed to be alone with my thoughts.

I settled back into the leather Chesterfield, giving a nod and a smile to the waitress hovering nearby as I gestured toward the empty whisky glass on the gleaming table.

"Another?" she asked with a smile.

"Please," I replied.

Walters was founded around the same time as SKA, but by then it had grown to 500 employees across six countries. The partners and senior managers were comfortably earning seven-figure salaries and reaching that level was well within my grasp if I stayed and worked hard over the next ten years. I had already earned a solid reputation within the firm, and such roles were almost guaranteed for me before I turned 40.

However, the relentless grind needed to stay on the hamster wheel should not be underestimated. The company was a pyramid, with a broad base filled by me and hundreds of others. Climbing up was possible, no doubt, but at what cost? Large corporate city firms were infamous for long hours, punishing KPIs, narcissistic management, and a readiness to cut jobs ruthlessly at the first sign of trouble.

Executive Search was a different kettle of apples. A more mature setting with a calmer pace of life. There were fewer fees to earn, but the ones that did come in were enough to make your eyes water. No KPIs, no micromanagement. The bigger cash would come faster, I could be on 7 figures within 3 years, but I would be giving up the chance to play on the main board of a multinational, with a gold key to the executive loo and my name on a private parking spot.

"Sir?"

I snapped back to the present. The waitress stood before me, shapely and poised, holding a large Chivas.

"Shall I put it here?" She asked, nodding toward the table.

"Please." I said, returning her smile with a polite one of my own.

She leaned forward to place the glass, her skirt inching slightly up her thighs as she did.

Two City Boys strolled past, loud and laughing, making their way to a nearby cluster of armchairs. The blond one dropped a heavy Bentley key ring onto the polished table with a deliberate clatter. The dark-haired one raised his hand, catching the waitress's eye. She straightened, clocked the key ring and the tailored suits, and made her way to them with a practiced sway, not sparing me so much as a glance.

I leaned forward, grabbed the drink, and drained it in one go. Then I reached into my wallet, pulled out three twenties, and laid them beside the empty glass.

As I stood to leave, a thought struck me:

What's the point of a parking space if you can't put a Bentley in it?

My mind was made up.

DIY

I took to Executive Search like a duck to water.

Actually, while you're here, can I get something off my chest? Why haven't our idioms caught up with the times? We're still banging on about ducks and water like it's 1850. Most of us live in flats now. When was the last time you saw a duck that wasn't crispy and aromatic?

Why not update it? "I took to it like a five-year-old to Fortnite." Or "like a Brexiteer to a vest and Stella"

And the whole "Don't put all your eggs in one basket?" Bollocks. Who's carrying eggs in baskets nowadays? Why not "don't save all your files on one hard drive?" That actually makes common sense.

We're not peasants anymore, we're professionals, and language should move with the times and reflect that. Honestly, it really gets my goat.

Our team secretary at SKA was a polite and demure Indian lady by the name of Kiara. We hit it off straight away. Whilst she reported directly to Simeon, one of her tasks was to format my CVs. When you send your CV to a headhunter, on the slim chance it doesn't go straight into the circular file, it will get passed to a secretary to add the company logo, remove your contact details, and generally get smartened and spruced up. This is called formatting.

My first few months at SKA were exceptionally busy. Simeon had a vast network of contacts, and opportunities flowed in easily. He introduced me to clients already investing heavily in interim solutions through our firm. I built relationships over lunches at The Ivy, rounds of golf at Muswell Hill Golf Club, or trips to Spearmint Rhino, securing their commitment to Exclusive Search assignments with £50,000 upfront payments.

Once I had taken a thorough job brief, I would then sit with the researchers and ensure they had everything they needed to move to the next, arguably the most important and certainly most testing part of the job, the headhunt

Chances are, if you've ever received a headhunt call or message, it wasn't from the headhunter themselves but from the unsung warriors of our trade, the researchers.

An Executive Search Researcher's job is to dig deep into industries and companies to unearth professionals like you who aren't openly looking but might be tempted by the right offer. Armed with LinkedIn, industry gossip, news articles, and well-placed whispers, they sift through reams of data and networks to build a hit list of potential candidates.

Then comes the delicate art of the initial contact. Whether it's a LinkedIn message crafted to flatter your ego or a discreet phone call timed to catch you at a weak moment, their mission is twofold: First, to figure out if you're actually a good fit for the role, client, and company; And second, if you are, to find out where you're most vulnerable in your current job, because knowing which bruises to punch makes it much easier to sell you on a supposedly better future.

Where were we? Ah yes, the burning bridges bit. (Again, a medieval idiom we still use, why not 'Don't wipe your hard drive?')

My first few months in Executive Search, and Burt had moved on, as he was wont to do. He had popped up in one of the aforementioned dotcoms and was busy building his team and spending pot loads of starry-eyed investors cash, a large proportion of it in my fees.

Now, I honestly can't remember the exact reason he came to be owing me this particular fee, but I do remember it was £45,000 plus VAT. We will have placed a senior finance professional in his team, and for some reason, Burt and I were locked in a fairly intense discussion about why he shouldn't (his position) or *absolutely fucking should* (mine) pay the invoice.

I do remember it being a grey area. Legally, according to our terms, the fee was due, but morally, it was questionable. More likely than not the candidate will have left his role within our money-back guarantee period, but, if they hadn't paid the bill within 7 days, as was blatantly and perfectly hidden somewhere on page 25 of our engagement contract, then the rebate clause is void.

If real estate is all about location, location, location, then recruitment is relationships, relationships, relationships. A good headhunter prays daily at that altar.

Burt, not just a solid mate but my golden goose, was one of those relationships. Giving up a single fee, juicy as it was, in favour of many more down the line was a no-brainer. Only a fucking idiot would dig his heels in over one deal because he'd promised his wife a brand spanking Audi TT.

Fucking idiot.

What I do remember, and what I've drilled into armies of junior recruiters ever since, is that from that day on, the tap was well and truly turned off. Professionally and personally.

And just to really rub salt in my self-inflicted wound, a few months later Burt took a permanent gig as CFO at a fast-growing dot-com search engine I'll call 'Yippee!'. His recruitment budget ran into the tens of millions of dollars per year.

Not a single cent of it ever troubled my bank account.

Of course, those relationships don't just refer to clients and candidates. They include the third 'C', which is our colleagues.

Let me take you back to Kiara, our hard-working team secretary. It was her first job out of college, and she quickly established herself as a valuable and well-liked member of the team. It's often said that your first job isn't to earn, but to learn, and I took it upon myself to help her grow professionally, to understand what it takes to build a career, not just hold down a job.

She reported directly to Simion, as I mentioned before, but I noticed he wasn't putting in the effort. Whenever she arrived a few minutes late or dashed out right at 5.30, he'd let it slide, missing the chance to politely but firmly reinforce what it means to show up properly in a corporate environment. I saw in Kiara the makings of a top performer, a gem, a diamond. In the rough, admittedly, but a diamond all the same.

One November afternoon, we were seriously up against it. A CEO from one of our US clients was flying in the next morning, and their HRD had just asked us to move our shortlist presentation forward, from tomorrow to that very evening, so she had time to review it before the big boss landed.

It was creeping up on 5.30, but I still had half a dozen CVs that needed formatting before Kiara could leave. This is recruitment. Success often comes from going the extra mile, from surprising and delighting your client, even if it means being late for your little sister's birthday party. Which, in this case, was exactly where Kiara was meant to be, judging by the way she kept glancing anxiously at the clock while hammering away at the keyboard.

"Kia-Ora," I said as I slid into the chair next to hers. She looked up at me with that theatrical exasperation she always gave me when I used the nickname I'd anointed her with.

"What did you get your sister for her birthday?"

"A ride-on car." She said. Her sister was turning six, and Kiara absolutely doted on her.

"OK. Here's the thing." I pointed through the glass window at the twinkling high-rises across the road. "Every one of those secretaries over there, the ones who leave bang on 5.30 to go to a party, they'll all be able to buy their sister a plastic car. This year, next year, the year after."

I paused, watching her face, hoping my point was landing.

"But." I continued, gently placing a cardboard file full of CVs next to her keyboard, "The ones who go the extra mile, who sacrifice a few hours of pop and crisps for the sake of client service. . ." I flipped open the file to reveal the stack of CVs, with a single Post-it on top reading: Formatted – Today.

"They're the ones who'll be buying their sister a real car on her 17th."

She stared at me. Blankly, deeply. Like she was actually absorbing it. My words of wisdom seemed to sink in.

I stood, still holding her gaze, slipped my jacket off the back of my chair and onto my shoulders.

"You, Kia-Ora, are a fucking star." I said, pointing a finger in the air for emphasis. She winced slightly at the language. She came from a kind, traditional family, far removed from the dog-eat-dog, cut-and-thrust of city life. But I made it part of my mission to polish that diamond, and yes, her daily exposure to real-life language was part of the education.

I paused at the office door, one hand on the handle.

"Come in half an hour later tomorrow, OK?" I said, and left.

The next morning, I was emerging from Holborn Tube into a dark, freezing London morning. The office was only a few minutes' walk, and I ducked my head and picked up the pace to escape the cold.

My phone rang. Simion.

I flipped it open. "Boss. What's happening?"

"Oh hi, Matt. It's Simion."

No shit, it says so on the screen. Lovely guy, gentle, mild-mannered, a bit fucking wet.

"Just wanted to let you know before you get in, Kiara won't be coming in. She just called and handed in her notice."

"Oh." I said, caught off guard. "Why?"

He hesitated. "She said… well, she said she needed a different pace of life. And erm… a different culture than SKA."

His words were still bouncing around in my head as I rode the lift to the 15th floor. I was angry. Disappointed. We'd lost a genuinely talented, ambitious colleague. One who'd realised our relaxed, patchy approach to her development wasn't going to take her where she wanted to go. Sure, I nudged her forward whenever I could, tried to stretch her, get her out of her comfort zone. But the bulk of her day-to-day was with Simion, and he was content to let her coast. Nine to five. Nine-ten, if we're being honest. He had a duty of care to challenge her, to push her out of her comfort zone, even if it meant stepping out of his own.

He hadn't even given her a nickname.

I beeped myself through the office door and barrelled past reception, heading straight for my desk.

We were going to need a new secretary. And this time, I thought, as I dropped into my chair and pulled the cardboard file toward me, she reports to me.

I flipped it open, shaking my head at Simion's complete lack of self-awareness.

The CVs were inside. On top, right where I'd left it, was the Post-it note.

Only now, underneath my handwriting, there was a new line, unmistakably Kiara's perfect penmanship:

"Format your own fucking CVs.

YOU.

FUCKING.

CUNT."

Prague Baby

I spent my days (and far too many evenings) talking to C-suite leaders about all the things that career ladders represent: Career progression, team growth, international expansion, strategic planning, budgeting, relocation packages.

And slowly, I began to realise. None of those milestones would ever apply to me. There's something quietly magnetic about the corporate ladder. The titles. The structure. The next step. None of these applied to me in my current role in Executive Search. Yes, I might get busier. More clients, maybe even hire a couple of researchers to help manage the load. But the job itself would remain the same. A client needs a CFO. I find one. Ideally just in time for the next brief to land. Rinse, repeat. Day after day. Until retirement.

My degree was in International Business and Foreign Languages. I spent 18 months living in France as part of the course and loved every minute.

That time abroad had planted a seed. Over time, it grew. I began looking into opportunities with international recruitment firms, ones with real scope for overseas moves, larger teams, new challenges. A place where the ladder was still in sight.

When a CFO needs a new role, she calls a specialist finance recruiter. Sometimes the recruiter may have a further specialism, such as only recruiting CFOs within aerospace, or telecoms, or retail. But when a recruiter starts feeling the itch to move, there's only one kind of specialist they can call.

The Rec-to-Rec.

Recruiters for recruiters.

A niche within a niche.

I had fielded a few calls from Rec to Recs in the past and had saved the names of the ones with whom I had had the best experience. One overcast afternoon in late January, when the office was quieter than usual, I hid myself in one of our meeting rooms, and dialled the number of the one I had selected to represent me.

Serena Perrera of Perrera Associates. If I was going to work with a Rec 2 Rec I wanted one whose name was above the door, whose door was only a few minutes from my office, and if she looked anything like her Linkedin picture then all the better.

A few days later, at an hour conveniently scheduled to fall over the lunch period, I arrived at their offices, was shown to a meeting room. Almost as soon as I had sat down, she entered. Impossibly polished. Glossy jet-black hair and a perfectly tailored blazer. "Matt." She said, as I stood to shake her hand. Her smile was warm, her grip confident, and she smelled expensive. Immediately, I felt underdressed, and over-Northern.

"So, what's prompting the curiosity?" she asked, like this was all perfectly normal, like this wasn't a recruiter to recruiter interviewing another recruiter about being recruited into a recruitment company.

An hour later, I was back on the street, practically giddy at the possibilities unfolding in front of me. Prague. I repeated the name to myself as I bounced down the pavement like some overcaffeinated tourist. Prague, Prague, Prague, Prague, Prague. I'd never been, but I'd heard only good things: Medieval gothic architecture, cheap beer, cheap everything, and that Cold War mystique you get from reading too much Le Carré. Spies, cobblestones, and Pilsner. What more could one ask?

The company had sounded promising too. Offices dotted across Eastern Europe, backed by deep-pocketed American investors. Technically, it was a job board, not a recruitment consultancy. One of the dot-com darlings that had survived the crash and was now setting its sights on a proper expansion push. They didn't do recruitment, but they wanted to.

That's where I came in. My mission would be to build a traditional consultancy, bricks and mortar as we liked to call it, alongside the shiny online job ad platform.

And it made perfect sense. The very same HR directors and functional leads who decided whether or not to advertise a role were often the ones who turned to headhunters when the hire was more senior, sensitive, or complicated. Why not offer them both options?

Better still, we had an ace up our sleeve. Every time someone sent their CV in response to a job ad, it landed quietly in our database. We were sitting on hundreds of thousands of active candidate profiles. A ready-made black book. An embarrassment of potential riches. All I had to do was build the team and spin all that beautiful data into gold. Ideally without getting too sidetracked by the beer.

Of course, there was the small matter of actually landing the job first.

Formality, I told myself. I was thirty, at the peak of my recruitment career, sharp as I'd ever been. And I had never missed anything I had set my sights upon. Twelve GCSEs, ten at A*. Captain of the First XV. Head boy. First-class honours degree. RAF pilot. A headhunter with a name that kicked down doors.

They would not simply offer me the job. They would tie it to a stone altar and throw its still beating heart at my feet!

They didn't offer me the job.

They gave it to my best friend.

So I made sure he had a car crash.

Now, I get that may be a little too much info to take in at one time. Not your fault, I have interwoven a few timelines here. Let me rewind a tad and we can explore together what really happened between the interviews and the crash.

My first encounter with the company came via a video call with the Group CEO. An hour-long conversation conducted over the ever-temperamental medium of Skype. To my surprise, I thoroughly enjoyed it. For someone with a personality such as mine, the rare opportunity to speak uninterrupted about one's own brilliance is a deeply indulgent pleasure, bordering on the therapeutic.

My interviewer, Norman, was a warm and affable Scotsman, the kind of man whose charm felt entirely natural. He spoke of the company with more depth and texture than Serena had previously offered. It had been founded five years prior, underpinned by the capital of both a VC firm and a benevolent American investor with a particular fondness for two things: Technology ventures and Eastern Europe. We, conveniently, represented both.

Their core business was an online job board operating across the Baltics, as well as Poland, the Czech Republic, and Hungary, with further ambitions stretching toward Romania and Türkiye. Yet the grander plan, what I'd been invited to help build, was not digital alone. It was to craft a recruitment company from the ground up in each of these markets. That meant assembling teams of consultants and researchers, owning the sales strategy, leading from the front, nurturing existing clients, and evangelising the brand across new frontiers.

It would also involve long evenings spent drinking frosty, cheap Czech beer and flirting with impossibly attractive waitresses in candlelit Prague taverns.

I shook myself gently back to reality, recognising that particular scene had been the invention of my own imagination, not part of Norman's official job description.

It was, in every sense, a pioneer's brief. The kind of role that invited equal measures of risk and excitement. As Norman detailed the operational challenges, I was already picturing myself in the role.

The second stage followed just a few days later. Serena had called that same afternoon, her tone bright and positive. Norman, she said, had been impressed. The next step would be a meeting with a few of the investors, who, understandably, wanted to meet the person about to pour a hundred grand's worth of their capital into the bars of Prague. I accepted without hesitation.

Once again, I found myself at my desk, smoothing out a few Post-it notes on the top right of my monitor. They were covered in quick scribbles: Key figures, polished soundbites, and the names of the five individuals I was about to meet, mental flashcards for what felt like a particularly high-stakes quiz.

They began to appear on screen, one by one. A ginger, a bear, a bookworm, a kindly aunt, and one who bore an uncanny resemblance to General Zod from Superman II. It was a more demanding hour than the first. A barrage of questions came at me from every direction, each laced with a distinct agenda, each delivered with a unique flavour of curiosity, caution or scepticism. I was careful not to play favourites, not to overlook the silent one, to land my punches cleanly while keeping my guard up.

By the time we reached the ceremonial waves and polite thank-yous, I was spent. I'd given everything I had. But as the hour had moved on, and I learned more about their hopes for the business, I realised something: I genuinely wanted this job. A real, pressing, almost physical sense of need. This was no longer just a new role and new company, but a complete change of my life as I had known it up to this moment.

I shut the laptop with a quiet click, leaned back in my chair, and reached for the bottle of whisky I'd placed on the desk earlier, anticipating this moment. I poured myself a generous measure.

The next day was Saturday. I figured it'd be midweek before I heard anything, there'd been a lot of stripes on that call, plenty of packed diaries to align.

I was down at the stables, the ones where my wife kept the horse I'd given her as a wedding present. Oh, did I forget to mention? That wine-drinking girlfriend I mentioned earlier had since been promoted.

She spent most weekends at the yard, and I'd drop in occasionally, either to keep her company or take Bismarck out over the fields for a few jumps. I was leaning over a stable door, admiring the way she moved as she bent to scoop a mixture of hay and horseshit into a bucket, when my phone buzzed in my pocket. It was Selena.

"Hey! Hi." I said, stepping away from the horses toward a quieter patch of the yard.

"Matt, hi." She purred. "Sorry to interrupt your Saturday, but I've already got the feedback. Is now a good time?"

"Er, yes, sure. Go ahead. Fire away."

"OK, well. . . look, it's probably not quite the news you were hoping for…"

My heart sank. Had to be the ginger one. What a ridiculous interview question anyway: If you could have one superpower, what would it be? I'd said China, because I like the food. I thought it showed I could stay witty under pressure.

"…but it's interesting," Selena continued.

"OK," I said. "I'm. . . interested."

By then I'd reached my car. I opened the passenger door, grabbed the pack of cigarettes from the seat, lit one, and leaned against the bonnet, bracing myself for the full picture.

"It was close," she went on. "But in the end, they gave it to another English guy. He's married to a Czech," she added, "and they're moving there anyway."

I was half-listening, sightly distracted by the view of my wife in the distance as she bent over the stable floor again, clearing up the last of the straw and manure.

"There's a but," Selena said.

You're not wrong, I thought, admiring the heroic effort her jodhpurs were putting in.

"They were wondering if you'd be open to doing the same role, just in Budapest."

My insides did a little somersault. Budapest! Yes. Absolutely. Budapest? Budapest, baby! We're all off to Bu Da Pest!

Where the fuck is Budapest?

Where the fuck is Budapest?

Budapest, jewel of the Danube and capital of Hungary, sits neatly at 47.4979° North, 19.0402° East. That puts it smack in the middle of Europe, a bit East of Vienna, West of Transylvania, and just landlocked enough that your winters will come early and leave late. Straddling the Danube River, the city is split into two: Hilly, historic Buda on one side and flat, buzzing Pest on the other.

Like many cities in our continent, it was the Romans who first set up shop Around the 1st century AD, they founded a city called Aquincum in what is now Óbuda. It had heated baths, amphitheatres, and wine from the Carpathian basin.

As they did, they eventually packed up, and a revolving door of tribes came through, until the Magyars arrived in the 9th century. These guys were serious about settling down, and under Chief Árpád, they laid the foundations of the Hungarian state. Buda became the king's hangout, while Pest grew into a gritty, money-making marketplace.

By the 13th century, things took a dark turn when the Mongols showed up and flattened the place. King Béla IV, in a move straight out of the 'too little, too late' playbook, ordered castles and walls built after the invasion. Still, to his credit, it worked the next time someone came knocking.

Fast-forward to the 15th century, and King Matthias Corvinus turned Buda into a Renaissance hotspot, books, science, and more wine, the whole deal. Then, in 1541, the Ottomans arrived and thought it looked like a nice place to stay. They brought coffee, Turkish baths, little storage boxes you put at the foot of your bed, and the kind of architectural flair that still survives today.

The Habsburgs kicked them out in 1686, declared it theirs, and spent the next two centuries adding Baroque charm to the architecture. By the 19th century, Pest was booming with industry, and in 1873, the cities of Buda, Óbuda, and Pest finally became Budapest.

The late 1800s were glorious. They built bridges, boulevards, and the world's second-oldest Metro line. Although at the time I suppose they saw it as the world's second newest Metro line. Then the 20th century showed up with two World Wars, Soviet occupation, and one revolution that was brave, tragic, and ultimately crushed.

Communism brought grey buildings, long queues, and a national obsession with pickling things. But by 1989, Hungary kicked the Soviets out, shrugged off the hangover, and set about rebuilding again.

Today, Budapest is a city of thermal baths, ruin pubs, and jaw-dropping architecture. It's romantic, gritty, elegant, weird, and still slightly confused about which side of the river is better.

My office was in Pest, just a short walk from the hotel the company had booked for my first three months in the city. I'd been in the role for a month already and was thoroughly enjoying the new job, challenging, engaging, exactly the sort of change I'd been hoping for.

The evenings, though, were a different story. Quieter. Lonely even. My wife and I had agreed that I'd head out first, get settled and start quickly, while she stayed behind to wrap things up: Sell the house, tie up loose ends, and follow me out as soon as she could.

We wrote to each other. Not hurried emails dashed off between meetings, but letters, real letters. The kind you fold with care and press to your lips before sending.

Mine were born each day at the same table outside my favourite bar, beneath the crooked shade of a fig tree that never quite kept the sun away. I would sit there in the hush, away from the city's noise, pouring my heart onto the page.

They were long letters, tender and aching, recounting our days, yes, but also whispering of the ache of being apart. They carried the weight of our love, raw and unguarded, and the quiet sorrow that crept in when night fell without each other.

We dreamed on those pages, sketched a life we hadn't yet lived. A future thick with laughter. Children with her eyes, grandchildren with my laugh, and a stableful of horses.

It was a Friday morning in the old office, the original office, as we had just signed the lease on a sleeker, more spacious place across town. Barely a month into the move and already the first green shoots of growth were pushing through: New clients, fresh revenue, a real feel of progress. Norman was pleased with me. The investors were smiling. I, too, felt quietly triumphant.

I sat on an upturned bin. We had quite literally run out of chairs. My perch was wedged at the corner of a four-person table already groaning beneath six of us. But no one complained. These were the good days, messy, yet going in the right direction.

I was deep into drafting a proposal, a recruitment campaign for a team of software engineers at a newly arrived Indian tech firm. The kind of assignment that would really move us forward in a quantum leap. Focused, I barely noticed Andika, our incredibly fragrant Office Manager, as she sashayed towards me. With a look that danced somewhere between amusement and pity, she dropped an envelope onto my keyboard. Her eyes said it all before she turned to glide away: *It's from your wife but look at what you could have won.*

I slid the letter aside. Work first. Numbers, margins, projections. Once satisfied, I pushed back from the table, bin scraping against the pine scented wooden floor, and finally opened the letter.

I remember standing as I read it, the noise of the office dimming around me. I have no memory of anything beyond the first paragraph. Though I would read those words again and again in the days to come, nothing else ever stayed. Just the beginning.

My dearest Matt

I hate myself for writing this. I'm not coming. I'm moving in with Robert. We've been together for some time, if I'm honest, since before you left. You're a wonderful person. You deserve better than me, and you'll find it. I'll sell the house and send you everything. I don't want any of it. Please don't write back. Don't call me.

hsgg, jihd3i oiuf4hf, jgsshg, shdh ey koei neh ...

The rest was nonsense, like a radio slipping out of range.

I'm standing in front of Norman. He is seated behind his desk, in his spacious office. Sitting on a real chair, the fucking show-off. A moment before, the letter was in his hand. Now it is resting on the mahogany of his table, and he is searching my face for a clue as to what the heck I am about to do. Later, much later, a couple of years down the road, he told me he thought I would resign, terminate the adventure in its infancy, fly back to prioritise my marriage.

The thought had never crossed my mind. My life was here, and I would rebuild it piece by piece without her. But I thought it wise to let the boss know why his Country Manager was a ball of tears and snot, and why I could be reached, should need be, for the rest of the day, at my bar, in the square, under the tree.

To be honest, I can't quite remember how I made it through the weekend. Most of it disappeared into a fog of whisky and silence, anything to dull the throb of my own numbness. By Monday morning, I was functional enough to drag myself back to the office. Still hollow. Still pissed off and ashamed. But the initial shock, that sledgehammer to the face, had faded into something quieter. Something survivable.

I stood at the bottom of the wrought iron staircase, the one that curled up to our first-floor landing. The office was tucked inside a former apartment block, the kind with a central courtyard and rusting balconies tracing the perimeter.

I paused to light a cigarette, the flick of the lighter loud in the morning stillness. The smoke was halfway out of my lungs when Norman materialized beside me, his hand already reaching toward the pack.

"Give us one of those." He said casually.

I held out the packet. He plucked a Marlboro from the crumpled cardboard and placed it between his lips. I lit it for him without a word. He took a long draw, exhaled like he was letting go of something heavy, then turned to me.

"How are you?" he asked, and I heard the real question in his voice. Not a formality, genuine concern lived behind his eyes.

"Shit." I said. "Empty."

He nodded, letting the silence stretch. I took another drag.

"But... I'm better than I was. Just..." I hesitated. "It was a massive shock, that's all. I'm not going anywhere, if that's what you're asking."

"I'm heading to Prague this afternoon," he said. "Couple of days with Jon. You should come. Change of scenery might do you good."

I blinked. Prague. I'd always wanted to go. My diary was light, nothing that couldn't be handed off to one of the consultants. And Jon, Jon with the Czech wife, Jon who'd taken my job but somehow managed to become a friend anyway, we spoke almost daily but had never met in person.

"Yeah," I said. "Yeah, why not? Thanks, Norman. What time's the flight?"

"No flight," he said, grinning. "Taking the Saab."

He'd just got it, a sleek, black 9-3 convertible with far too much horsepower. A five-hour drive across polished, EU-funded motorways. It sounded perfect.

He took one last drag from his cigarette, then flicked it to the ground and crushed it under his heel, the ember dying with a hiss.

"Head back to the hotel," he said, starting up the staircase, footsteps echoing. "Grab a bag. Meet me back here, and we'll hit the road."

Speaking of cars, let me walk you through the rusting piece of shit currently wasting away in the underground car park of the hotel I was staying in.

'Piece of shit' wasn't quite the terminology used in the official job offer from Selena. In the letter, it was described, rather grandly, as a fully-expensed-company-car.

I remember calling her just minutes after reading the contract, thrilled to accept and already itching to ask about the budget for the vehicle, imagining myself flicking through glossy dealership brochures.

She sounded. . . caught off guard.

"Erm, that's not exactly the process." She said. "They already have the cars. And. they're a bit old, apparently."

"Okay." I replied, cautiously.

"But," she continued, gamely trying to put a positive spin on it, "Norman did say he doesn't think they have long left. So when they, um, conk out, I suppose." She gave a light, awkward chuckle. "The plan is to replace them with much nicer models."

I paused, considering. "Alright, fair enough," I said, with a shrug she couldn't see. Slightly disappointed, sure, but this was just a minor footnote in a much larger, life-changing chapter.

A bit old? Bless Selena and her poetic licence

I'd just arrived at the hotel and needed to deposit a sleeve of cigarettes into the car for the road trip. I fished the keys from my pocket and, my thumb flicked around for the unlock button, before I remembered that my vehicle had been manufactured roughly a decade before remote entry was a thing.

I did it the old-fashioned way: Metal key into the lock. The turn was accompanied by a squeaky crunch I hadn't heard before, but it didn't surprise me.

The car was a 20-year-old Astra. Once upon a time it had been black, but two decades of Hungarian summers had left it a weary patchwork of mismatched greys. It was covered in peeling stickers bearing the name of the company website, some of which, I was fairly certain, were structurally important.

I leaned inside to deposit the cigarettes. The interior smelled like a blend of wet dog and spilt milk. Like I said, far from ideal, but I wasn't going to cry over it.

I backed out of the car and closed the driver's door with the two-handed technique I'd already learned: A sort of firm push followed by a hip check, which was necessary to stop it flopping open again.

I was crouched beside the car, studying a puddle of unknown gunk peeking out from beneath the front wheel arch. It looked suspiciously fresh. My phone buzzed in my jacket pocket. I fished it out. Norman.

"Norman, hi."

"Matt, hey, listen, I completely forgot." He said, that soft Highland lilt coming through. "After Prague, I'm heading straight up to Warsaw for a couple of days. Totally slipped my mind, but yeah, you'll have to take your own car back. That alright?"

"Yeah, sure." I said, glancing at the fluid on the asphalt and hoping it wasn't from anything too crucial.

"Brilliant. I'll see you up there. Don't forget your passport!"

"Cool." I said and hung up. I wrestled the driver's door open again and collapsed into the seat.

What a car crash

"You're fucking joking!"

It was Jon, on speakerphone, as I barrelled through the Slovak countryside in my clattering relic of a car.

"She's holding together alright," I said, just as we hit a bump. The passenger window dropped clean into the door with a thunk and vanished. "Can't push her past 80, though, so I'll be a while. Oh, by the way, one of my windows just disappeared"

"Mate, I wouldn't even drive mine across Prague." Jon shot back. His was the same ancient Astra, same rust, same cough in the engine, shitly identical except his stickers were in Czech.

Jon was a proper petrolhead. Cars mattered to him. He was also a sharp-looking guy, always in a tailored suit, watch gleaming, hair just so. He took his image seriously. I genuinely thought he'd rather be spotted getting out of one of Prague's many prostitutes than the wheezing eyesore he'd been saddled with.

While I'd taken the inheritance in my stride, for Jon it had almost been a deal breaker. It was only Norman's solemn promise that as soon as it needed any type of work done, that would be the time to retire and replace it, that had led to him accepting the job.

The lush Czech countryside was starting to give way to the industrial outskirts of Prague. The Astra seemed to give a sigh of relief as I eased off the throttle to match the city speed.

I picked up my phone again and hit redial.

"Wotcha!" Said Jon, cheerfully.

"Mate, quick one, I'm coming up to the office, any space outside to park?"

"Hold on." He said, as I heard him straining to stand and peer through the office window.

"Yep, there's room behind mine, bang outside. Where are you?"

"Five mins I reckon."

"Alright cool, I'll pop down and have a fag with you."

I hung up and tossed the phone onto the passenger seat. Excited about meeting my mate for the first time. His mention of a cigarette had triggered a Pavlovian response in me, and I wound down the window and lit on up for the final drive in.

Since this first magical visit I must have spent months in Prague, and it is one of my favourite places in the world.

It all began when a group of prehistoric humans stumbled across a lovely patch of land by the Vltava River and thought, This would make a great place to settle down and invent really strong beer.

By the 9th century, attracted by the smell of hops, the Přemyslid dynasty had moved in. They built Prague Castle and even more breweries.

In the 14th century, Charles IV showed up, and things really kicked off. He was a Holy Roman Emperor and professional overachiever. He founded Charles University in 1348, commissioned Charles Bridge, and created New Town, which is still called 'New' despite being older than most countries. Charles made Prague the third-largest city in Europe and also the place with the highest per-capita rate of pointy towers.

Then came the 15th century, and with it, religious chaos. A local priest named Jan Hus dared to suggest that maybe the Church was being a bit greedy. Naturally, he was invited to a council, given a nice warm stake to stand on, and burned alive. This made people extremely cross. So cross, in fact, that they invented the Hussite Wars. Prague became a theological boxing ring, and everyone got very good at building fortifications and ducking.

In 1526, the Habsburgs inherited Bohemia, turned up with fabulous moustaches and even better tanks, and decided to stick around. The city was now part of the Austrian Empire, and the locals presumably sat around eating Swiss rolls with their beer.

And then came 1618, the year Prague invented its most famous political tradition: Defenestration, the posh Latin word for the act of chucking someone out of a window to express disagreement with their views in a particularly gravity-based fashion. In this case, a group of angry Protestant nobles tossed two Catholic officials and their secretary out of the third-floor window of Prague Castle. The three men fell about 70 feet. Miraculously, all survived, reportedly because they landed in a great big pile of shit. This incident triggered *the Thirty Years' War,* which was, as the name suggests, neither short nor friendly. At least, to the relief of primary school teachers across the country, it avoided being awarded the title of *the great big pile of shit war*.

While Prague has moved on from the airborne removal of political rivals, some modern leaders still find glass panes irresistible when settling disputes. Prague may have started the trend, but Russia seems determined to keep it alive.

Back in Prague, the Habsburgs rebuilt the city in high Baroque style, turning it into a beautiful place to be quietly miserable under imperial rule. By the 19th century, Czech nationalism was bubbling up again. Poets, scholars, and pub philosophers worked hard to revive the Czech language, which had been politely pushed aside in favour of German. The city was becoming Czech again.

In 1918, after World War I, Czechoslovakia was born, and Prague became its capital. It was a good time to be a new republic. For about two minutes. Then the Nazis arrived in 1939 and really fucked everything up. The city was occupied until 1945, when it was liberated by the Soviets, greeted by locals who presumably stood cheering and reassuring themselves that absolutely nothing could possibly go wrong from now on.

In 1948, communists staged a coup, and the Cold War era began. In 1968, the Prague Spring brought a wave of hope and reform. It lasted just long enough for everyone to get excited before tanks rolled in to crush it. Soviet style.

But Prague does not stay quiet forever. In 1989, the Velvet Revolution changed everything. No blood, no tanks, just demonstrations by crowds big enough to suggest to the Soviets that it might be a good idea to keep the tanks in the garage this time.

In 1993, Czechoslovakia became Czech, and Slovakia. The borders were drawn up by a committee overseen by the United Nations, in a move designed to ensure that each country ended up with exactly the same amount of strip clubs.

I rounded the final corner of my journey and saw Jon ahead of me, enjoying a cigarette on the pavement next to which stood his embarrassment of a car.

A thought came to me. Quite a nasty, stupid one. Nasty stupid thoughts have a habit of popping into my head, as I am sure they do into yours. Normally, a few seconds of rational logical thought has time to do battle with the ridiculous one, and common sense prevails.

But, in this instance, by dint of what I was about to do, there weren't enough of those precious seconds to restore normality.

I pointed the nose of the Astra to line up and park gracefully behind Jon's and instead barrelled straight into it at about 20 miles per hour.

There was an almighty fucking bang, and a huge white airbag appeared in front of my face. My car stalled with a shudder, and his alarm started screaming at the injustice of a very vicious assault.

I gathered myself for a second, then reached down to retrieve my phone and cigarettes from the footwell, unfastened my seatbelt and got out.

Somebody had paused Jon. He was standing, completely motionless, his cigarette halfway to his mouth, surveying the scene.

I don't know much about motor mechanics, so I can only describe the scene as lots of parts that used to be front parts of my car, and lots of parts that used to be rear parts of his car, mashed together in a heap between the two. His car had been shunted forward about six feet and had come to a stop, thankfully, a few inches behind a very shiny Mercedes.

"Alright!" I said cheerfully.

"What. The. Fuck?" He managed to get out.

I turned to survey the scene.

"Oh that, yeah. Sorry mate. Brakes seemed to have failed."

"What the fuck?" Still the only part of him moving was his mouth, the cigarette still paused mid journey.

"Shit, yeah." I said. "Jon, looks like both of us are going to have to get brand new cars now."

Who would take a bribe?

A week had passed since my run-in with the Swiss roll mafia. I was at my desk, enjoying a rare moment of peace and actual thought. I'd been contemplating whether I could justify a walk across the office just to flirt with Andika when I felt a presence approaching.

I looked up just as the woman in question perched herself on the corner of my desk and leaned in, eyes glinting with mischief.

"Matt, I have a big ass," she said, voice low and deliberate.

"I'm sorry?"

"A big ass. For you."

I stared at her, scanning her face for any hint of what game she was playing and what I was supposed to say in response. Before I could figure it out, Vik breezed past, arms full of files.

"Put it away, Mr Foster." She called without stopping.

"She said she has a big ask." Vik added over her shoulder.

I turned back to Andika, trying not to let the disappointment register.

"You have a question for me?"

"Yes. It's about Bence."

Bence was our newest hire. I adored the guy. A small, shaven-headed Slovak who, like many of his generation, had fled the dead-end villages of the east for Budapest and the promise of city lights.

Ours was his second job in Hungary. He'd come from a boiler room scam, selling worthless penny stocks to gullible investors. He once told me about the day he left, the same day the authorities raided the place, flanked by a half-dozen Hungarian cops.

Bence and a few mates had been outside on a cigarette break, idling on the balcony as the raid crashed through the front door. They bolted. Left everything behind, phones, wallets, and the laminated scripts they'd repeated a hundred times a day.

He'd only been with us a few days, but I was already loving Bence The honesty. The energy. The fact that he actually gave a shit. But there was one problem.

"He stinks," Andika said flatly.

He fucking stank.

The kind of stink that made you reconsider shared cars and indoor spaces. His suit hung off him and his hair was cropped too close to the scalp. He was still transitioning between the fields of Slovakia and the high rises of the city.

I looked Andika in the eye and nodded. "Leave it with me. I'll sort it." She smiled with a wrinkle of the nose, then slid gracefully off my desk and wandered off.

Left alone, I leaned back and considered the problem. How do you tell a grown man he reeks?

Then the idea arrived.

"Vik!" I called across the office as I stood and grabbed my jacket. "Heading to my client meeting. Procter & Gamble."

I pitched it loud enough for her and most of the floor to hear.

Vik looked up, confused, eyes flicking to my calendar on her screen.

"Back in two hours." I added cheerfully, grabbing my car keys and striding out before she could challenge the lie.

I took the lift to the ground floor. Not to the basement, where my car dozed in the dark, but straight through the foyer and into the sunlight. Across the street, into Tesco Metro, I made my purchases and checked my watch.

One hour fifty-five to kill.

So I did the only reasonable thing. Turned the corner, found the square, dropped into my usual seat, and summoned a waitress.

Ninety minutes and two ice-cold pints later, I picked up my box of goodies and headed back.

Inside, I spotted Vik near the boardroom, phone to her ear, pacing like a nervous cat. My phone buzzed in my pocket. She saw me, hung up, and marched over, eyes fixed on the box in my hands.

"Where the hell have you been? You've got visitors."

I assumed it had been her calling me. "Tell you in a sec." I said, walking past her and onto the trading floor and the bank of desks where Bence sat.

"Hey kids!" I grinned, placing the box on the desk with theatrical flair. Eight pairs of eyes turned toward it like children on Christmas morning.

"Just came from a meeting with P&G." I announced. "Picked up a CFO role. They also gave us these toys." I gestured to the eight cans of Sure deodorant nestled inside the box.

"Help yourselves."

They pounced. The box was empty in seconds. Like pigeons on sick.

I looked directly at Bence. He held his can like it was the FA Cup.

"Thanks, boss." He said. Then, "What is it?"

"It's called deodorant, Bence. You spray it under your arms every day after your shower. You know. Your daily shower. It makes you feel amazing. Give it a try."

He stared at it like it was magic.

"Thanks, boss. I'm going to try it!"

I turned back to Vik, grinning.

"Now that's management, Viktoria." I murmured.

She narrowed her eyes, still half annoyed, half impressed. "They're in the boardroom."

"The Swiss Roll boys?" I asked.

She nodded.

I stepped into the room where Larry, Curly, and Moe were already seated in a neat row, three hulking shapes stuffed into overworked leather jackets, like a sofa with Turkey teeth.

"Gentlemen." I said, reaching out to shake three calloused hands in quick succession. I pulled out a chair, sat down, and laid a legal pad and pen in front of me.

"Mr. Foster." Larry said, his voice dry but polite. "Thank you for seeing us again."

I didn't have much fucking choice, did I? I thought.

"A pleasure." I replied.

"We've considered your proposal." He leaned forward, catching Moe's eye and giving him a slight nod. Moe responded with a dip of the head and reached down to the floor. When he rose again, he was holding an Adidas holdall. He placed it on the table with a muffled thud.

I tried not to let my unease show. The bag was big enough for a range of sharp kitchen implements or my girlfriend's head. I held my breath as Moe unzipped it, then shoved it toward me with thick fingers.

I glanced inside. Then at the three amigos. Then back again.

Stacks of US dollars. Fat, neat, banded bundles of them.

"$50,000." Moe confirmed helpfully.

"Erm." I said. I needed time to think here. "Erm." I said again, still more time.

Pull yourself together, Fozzy.

"Right. Well. Thank you, first of all. But… this isn't how we usually operate. Normally, we'd agree a contract, send an invoice, you wire the funds. This." I motioned to the sports bag, nudging it slightly back. "This isn't standard procedure."

Larry studied my face. After a pause that felt longer than it probably was, he spoke again. "Mr. Foster, invoices mean paperwork. Paperwork means taxes. Paperwork means your boss hears about this deal." His meaty hand was steady as he pushed the bag back toward me.

Then he turned to the one in the middle. "Oleg."

I watched as the Hulk unzipped his leather cocoon just enough to reach inside to his breast pocket. My pulse spiked, briefly. Ridiculous to think they'd offer me fifty grand and then shoot me a second later, but still. I exhaled when his hand emerged with something small, dark, and velvet.

He placed a box gently on the table. Opened it with theatrical precision and pushed it toward me.

Inside, catching glints of Budapest sunlight slashing through the blinds, was the most stunning Audemars Piguet I'd ever seen. I recognized it instantly, a Royal Oak Selfwinding. It practically sang.

"It is present. To say thank you." Someone said, I didn't catch who. My eyes were locked on the watch.

I leaned back. Pulled my attention away from the glinting lure on the table. Looked at the men.

There was no way we could take the cash. The CFO wouldn't even entertain the idea. No way we could take the project either, who accepts a job where the previous guy's CV doubles as his obituary? And no way I could pocket the bribe and keep it secret from the company.

But if we didn't take the brief, then I definitely couldn't keep the gift either.

I looked at them, then silently closed the box.

Buy low sell high

I'm no longer in Budapest, as you know, and since these events unfolded I've spent a fair stretch of time in Dubai. This feels like the perfect moment to explain how I came to no longer be there at all.

We've already covered the structure of the company's ownership: I held a handful of shares, as did Norman, Jon, and a couple of other country managers. The real control, however, rested with the Venture Capitalists, who held the lion's share.

Venture Capitalists, or VCs as everyone calls them, are professional risk-takers. They don't make anything. They don't manage anyone. They don't solve problems or write code or post anything physical to anyone. What they do is take other people's money and bet it on people who might create something that changes everything.

It works like this. VCs raise what's called a fund, usually hundreds of millions, sometimes billions. That money comes from investors known as limited partners. These include pension funds, family offices, universities, insurance firms, and even sovereign wealth funds. These institutions are looking for higher returns than they'd get from safer investments, and they trust the VCs to go out and find the next big thing.

Once the fund is raised, the hunt begins. VCs meet with hundreds of startup founders, listen to their pitches, dig into their slide decks, test their products, and size up their markets. Most of these founders will not get a penny. But a few will. And what a pretty penny it can be. If a VC believes in the business or in the person running it, they offer funding in exchange for equity, which means a slice of ownership. This is usually somewhere between 10 and 30 percent depending on the size of the cheque and how early the investment is.

That is where it starts. The cash hits the startup's account, and the clock begins ticking.

Here is the part that matters: venture capital is not about building sustainable businesses. It is about creating high-growth companies that can be sold quickly. Ideally within five to ten years.

The whole model is based on the idea of the exit. That is when the company either gets acquired by a bigger fish with deeper pockets or goes public in an IPO. That is when everyone cashes out: the founders, the early employees, and most importantly, the Venture Capitalists.

Until that moment, they are on the ride. VCs usually take a board seat. They offer guidance, introductions, and strategy tips. Sometimes they are helpful. Sometimes they just slow things down. But they are always present and always watching. Their job is not just to invest but to protect and grow the investment.

It is a numbers game. Most of the startups they back will fail. That is expected. Venture funds do not rely on every investment being successful. They rely on a few of them being wildly, explosively successful. If they invest in ten companies, five might collapse within two years. Two or three might muddle along, barely returning the original investment. But one, just one, might become a unicorn, a billion-dollar company. That one win covers the losses and makes the fund a success.

The incentives are clear. VCs want speed, growth, and traction. The faster a company can scale, the faster it becomes valuable. That is why so many VC-backed startups operate in a constant state of sprint. The pressure is relentless. Hire fast. Build fast. Raise more money. Capture the market before anyone else does. If you burn through a few people along the way, so be it.

Which brings us to what it feels like to work in one of these companies.

At first, it is intoxicating. There is energy and buzz. Everyone is hustling, sharing ideas, staying late, living off caffeine, beer and Marlboro lights (OK maybe just me). It feels like you are building something that matters. But underneath the energy, there is something colder. A quiet truth that nobody says out loud.

If this company succeeds, we all leave.

That is the paradox of VC-backed startups. If it fails, the company shuts down and everyone gets fired. If it succeeds, if the service takes off, if the valuation climbs, and if a big player comes knocking, the company gets sold, the founders move on, and everyone leaves. That is not a bug in the system. It is the system.

From the first day you walk in the door, the business is designed for exit.

It is like being in a marriage where both partners are already planning the divorce. Everyone is committed but only for a while. You give your best, knowing the end is baked into the beginning.

It is exciting. It is exhausting, but it is temporary.

When you work inside one of those companies, you learn quickly: no one is sticking around forever.

Not the founders, not the investors, and certainly not you.

And so it happened: Month by month, year by year, we quietly engineered our own redundancy. We had not only met the targets the VCs had set, we had exceeded them. By this point, Norman, suitably impressed by how fast I had built the Hungarian business, had handed me a regional role. My life became a blur of boarding passes and hotel check-ins.

Latvia, Lithuania, Estonia, Poland, the Czech Republic, Hungary, Poland and Romania. Under my control, all of them were thriving, each turning healthy profits for the investors. Our recruitment firms were humming, and the online job boards we ran dominated their local markets.

The thought of selling the business began to creep into view, faint at first, then inevitable. It was time to look for the next adventure. That's when Dream, one of the UK's recruitment heavyweights, appeared on the horizon. Like most corporate giants, they had taken their time deciding on a new strategic direction. Eventually they saw it: the untapped potential of Eastern Europe's emerging markets, and they wanted in.

I honestly can't recall whether it was Jon or me who took the phone call. On the other end was Ricardo Frodo, Dream's International Director – a brilliant, pint-sized Marxist with a proven track record of making things happen. His mission was to add the Iron Curtain countries to his empire, and between Jon and me, he saw the fastest route to hotwire his expansion.

Whoever he spoke to first, the result was the same. One of us recommended the other. We were a package deal. Take both of us, or take neither.

We agreed to meet somewhere convenient for Ricardo, Jon, and me. It was decided on Poland – more specifically, the Sheraton in Warsaw. At the time, I had no idea that a couple of years later, I'd be the reason the entire hotel was evacuated in the dead of night. Fire engines ringing the building, their lights slicing through the darkness, while bewildered businessmen from half a dozen countries milled around outside – some accompanied by the evening's… temporary companions.

What happened was this. I had been with Dream for a couple of years, my remit once again growing from a single country to an entire region. Poland was again under my wing, and on the evening in question I was visiting with a colleague named Craig Port. Craig led our Learning and Development team. My job was to manage the daily output of our consultants, while his was to make sure they were trained, confident, and armed with the skills to deliver the results I demanded.

Craig was a few years younger than me, infuriatingly good-looking, and brilliant company. We shared the same recreational priorities: Drinking far too much and attempting to charm Eastern European cocktail waitresses.

That evening, we agreed to meet in the hotel bar. He had flown in from our London head office, I from Budapest. I spotted him crossing the foyer, the eyes of most of the female staff following him as if on a string. He reached me just as I drained the last of my second pint, threw his arms wide open, and we exchanged a hug with the obligatory manly backslap.

"Come on, mate." I said, freeing myself from his embrace. "Let's hit the casino. This money's not going to lose itself."

"Alright. I'll just drop my bag in my room and iron a shirt. See you back here in twenty."

I glanced at my watch. It was already eight o'clock, and we had a nine-a.m. start in the morning.

"Forget the ironing, mate. Use the shower trick."

"What's the shower trick?"

I could not remember the last time I had ironed a shirt while travelling. The method was foolproof: Hang a shirt inside the shower, crank the hot water on full, and by the time you stumbled back to your room, you would be greeted by a perfectly steamed, wrinkle-free shirt, ready for the next day.

I was impatient to get out. Jon had fabricated a reason to be in Warsaw that night too, and, being rather partial to the green baize, he was already across the road in the Golden Future Casino.

Craig and I met him in there, Craig's shower happily cascading away back in his room.

This particular casino was our favourite. As long as you were gambling, the free drinks kept flowing. Our game of choice that evening was blackjack, and we sat together as a trio, slowly getting toasted, and by turn winning and losing, but most importantly, enjoying each other's company.

We had about an hour left before the Casino's closing time of 3 am. Craig, sitting between me and Jon, was flagging. He was functioning, just, his eyes would close, and his head would dip before righting itself with a jolt. I leaned over and tapped Jon on the shoulder with a grin. He looked at me, rather blearily, and I gestured towards the large pile of chips in front of Craig. He nodded with a grin, and simultaneously, we both helped ourselves to a good proportion of Craigs, winnings, sliding them quietly towards our own piles.

The beer kept flowing, the cards kept coming. Every time Craig lost consciousness, Jon and I would relieve him of more of his winnings. Fighting back the urge to laugh out loud every time he looked in bemusement at his tiny pile of chips and pulled out his wallet to replenish it.

The waitress appeared at my shoulder with three ice cold pints of…Coke? She set them out in front of us and after a wry smile, shimmied away. Jon and I looked at each other in confusion. Coke? I turned to attract the waitress's attention to rectify the mistake and was greeted by the immaculately suited floor manager. He leaned towards me, and with a gesture drew my attention to the CCTV camera on the ceiling above us. I caught up. "Jon" I said. He looked at me. I took a good proportion of my chips and slid them back in front of Craig. Jon followed suit. The floor manager nodded and clicked his fingers, to summon the waitress, who arrived instantly with the 3 cold beers we had ordered.

They were to be the last of the evening, as the closing hour had arrived. We poured ourselves outside the casino and were greeted with the sight of hundreds of hotel guests, in various states of undress, standing outside the doors of our hotel. 3 fire engines illuminate the darkness with pulses of blue light.

The shower trick had served me faithfully in hotels across the world. Every hotel, in fact, except the Sheraton in Warsaw. There, it seems, if you leave the shower running while you slip across the road for a few hours of gentle gambling, it is entirely possible to set off the smoke alarm in your room, which in turn triggers the sprinklers in every room on your floor. And the floor above. And the floor below.

It also has the unfortunate side effect of earning you a lifetime ban from every Sheraton on the planet.

Sorry, Craig.

The 'bone doctor'

But let's rewind a couple of years. Outside the same Sheraton, in the same spot, having a cigarette with Jon. He had just met Frodo. I was due to meet him in less than fifteen minutes.

Jon had been interviewed for the role of Country Manager for their new Prague office, which he would be responsible for setting up. I had the same brief, but for Budapest. It was exactly the same challenge we had both accepted nearly five years earlier, only now we had in-country experience and ready-made teams of thirty consultants in each location from which we could cherry-pick the best.

Jon had struggled slightly in his interview. I aced mine. Not for any other reason than the fact that I had used those fifteen minutes to grill Jon on the exact questions I would be asked. By the time I walked in and shook Frodo's hand, the job was as good as mine.

We each received an offer the next day, with packages far higher than the ones we were leaving behind. Our experience had real value now.

We both resigned on the same day. It was surprisingly undramatic. The company was being split and sold in two parts: The online job boards and the traditional recruitment business would go their separate ways. Norman, to whom we resigned, would also be leaving. In situations like this, the new owners bring their own executives and management teams. Our departure was a clean break, and mutually beneficial.

After five years, I was ready for a change. On paper, it looked like a step backwards. I would be trading a regional role overseeing 200 consultants across Europe for a bare office in Budapest and the challenge of building it all from scratch again. This time, though, it would be for a far larger organisation. Yes, I had been at the top of the tree, but in truth that tree had been a sapling compared to the mighty oak I was about to join. My only hesitation was the culture.

The year I joined, the company was celebrating its 70th anniversary. It was a household name. The Cadbury's or Lea & Perrins of recruitment, known for its restraint, a far cry from the freewheeling rollercoaster I was stepping off. I could not help but wonder how they might react if I mentioned that one of my most memorable assignments at VCI had been recruiting a new editor-in-chief for Penthouse magazine.

That project had come through the wife of an expat friend, herself the CEO of the publishing house. He asked on her behalf if I would consider taking on the search. I practically bit his hand off. A week later, I was seated in the offices of Masthead Media, across the desk from his wife, pen poised to take down every detail of the brief. The place could only have existed in Hungary. Magazines lay scattered across tables, but the true showpieces were the walls: towering posters of centrefolds, blown up to life size. Behind the CEO, a sideboard displayed a box of "toys" sent for review.

The receptionists, I noted, were also frequent stars of the magazine's pages.

As we worked through the job description, I discovered the editor-in-chief did very little actual editing. That was the subeditors' domain. The role was essentially about presence—a PR figurehead, the face of the brand, the illusion, the fantasy. Candidates would include television presenters, film stars, and pop singers. No editing skills required, but stamina was essential. The job was a relentless carousel of events, launches, after-parties, and press calls, each designed to generate as many column inches as possible.

I loved every moment of the search and still count a few of those famous faces as friends today. During the assignment, I was invited to one of the magazine's parties. It was held in a sprawling apartment in the city centre, hired purely for the occasion. The evening slipped into the small hours on a tide of Veuve Clicquot. Amid the laughter and champagne, I caught myself wondering what the business case might be. It seemed little more than employees and models drinking fine champagne and grazing on canapés. Perhaps it was simply a perk, much like companies today installing dartboards and PlayStations in their break rooms.

At one point, I found myself in the kitchen, speaking to a striking brunette. "And what do you do?" I asked. "I am a bone doctor." She replied smoothly. "And you?"

"I'm a headhunter."

She tilted her head. "What is a headhunter?"

I switched to Hungarian.

"I am a fejvadász." Pronounced Fay Vod Ass.

Her eyes lit up. "Interesting. You are a favoured ass?"

I think I blushed. That was quite fruity language, I thought, for a doctor.

"Have you been in Budapest long?" she continued.

"Coming up to three years."

"Do you need anyone to… show you around?"

I considered for a moment, then answered rather naively. "No, I think I know the place quite well by now. It is not half as big as London."

She looked at me with mild surprise. "Your loss," she said, lifting her glass from the counter before gliding out of the kitchen. As she left, she brushed past Norman, who had just hurried in. I had invited him along; We were good friends by then and shared a fondness for enthusiastic socialising.

He glanced around to check she was out of earshot. "How did it go with Michelle?" he asked eagerly. "Who, the doctor?" I replied, puzzled at how he knew her.

"Doctor? What doctor?"

"Michelle," I said. "She's a bone doctor."

"She's an actress," he corrected. "The most famous mattress actress in Hungary. You didn't know?"

"She told me she was a bo—oh." The penny dropped. I looked past him into the vast living room just in time to see Michelle sweeping her coat from the stand and disappearing into the night. I stood there for a moment, wondering what might have interested her in me. Perhaps it was the accent. Perhaps the novelty of a Brit deep behind what was once the Iron Curtain. I glanced at my wrist to check the time.

Or perhaps it was the Audemars Piguet Royal Oak Selfwinding.

Honey and money

Perhaps my naivety was a blessing in disguise. I had just started seeing a captivating Hungarian woman I'd met at a Burns' Night supper in one of the city's grandest five-star hotels.

About a year earlier, I had joined the Freemasons, and Sir Rabbie Burns was something of a poster boy for us. That, and the promise of copious whisky, made it an unmissable occasion.

It was a bitter black night in late January. The ballroom shimmered under chandeliers, tartan and gold draped across every surface. My friends and I sat at a table for ten, glasses in hand, as all eyes turned to Norman. He stood on stage, magnificent in full Highland dress, swaying gently as he slurred his way through the Address to the Haggis. Among the crowd was my friend, Spiderman, the spy. I'll tell you more about how we met later. He was accompanied by his striking new girlfriend. She had brought along a single friend of her own, Ilona. From the moment we spoke, she was a revelation. She had lived in the UK and carried with her a lilting accent, a razor-edged wit, and that dry, ironic humour I had missed so much since leaving Blighty. I was smitten.

After a night of raucous conversation, flowing whisky, and suspiciously orange crap called "neeps," I found myself the next morning in my apartment, frying bacon and eggs for her as sunlight filtered weakly through the frost on the windows.

I will not linger on Ilona's story. We married, had two wonderful children, and later, not long after I returned to the UK, we divorced. Her life and privacy deserve respect.

But the spy's girlfriend... that is another matter entirely. I can't tell you who she was. I can tell you this much: she was not who she seemed.

What we do already know is that my friend's role in the defence of our realm involved him taking frequent trips to British Embassies and Consulates across Eastern Europe.

One such occasion was just before Christmas, so a month or so before the Burn's supper. He was walking through one of the offices buried deep inside the British Embassy in Bucharest, Romania, guided by a more junior technician who had unearthed a particularly disconcerting series of high frequency radio waves that really should have had no place in the building and that he wanted Sam to check out. As he passed by the desks of various local typists, administrators and data inputters, one of them, a stunning six-foot blonde beauty, with piercing green eyes and a Jessica rabbit figure, turned to her nearest neighbour, and indicated towards my mate. "Who is that?" She asked. Followed by "Oh my God he is gorgeous."

Now, let's get one thing straight here. He was one of my dearest friends. If she would have said, *my God he has a great sense of humour,* I would have agreed with her in a heartbeat, but of course, she wasn't to know that. Or, *Oh God I bet he can down ten pints of Boddington's in the embassy bar then lie back on the nearest table and light his farts*, then I couldn't have disagreed with her. But. . . Gorgeous?

For a start, what with he being about 4 feet tall, I am surprised she saw him passing her desk in the first place. His hair looked as if he wasn't quite on top of all the electrical gear he worked with and was constantly being electrocuted.

In terms of an unlikely couple, if you saw them walking down the street hand in hand you would assume she had captured him running wild and was returning him back to his cage.

My friend had known the Amazon's desk neighbour for a while, and he was very quickly whispered the news that Marianna found him alluring on a physical level. The next thing we all know, they are an item, she has resigned her job in the embassy. moved to Hungary and taken up residence in his enormous villa that the British taxpayer was paying for. This is all within a month. They settled in together, and the four of us became inseparable, often found together on nights out.

Mariann started to gradually stay away, overnight, in foreign countries. first for a night, then a couple, then longer periods which could bleed into weekends. On one occasion I questioned my friend as to the nature of these travels. "Oh, it's just work." he said. "I don't mind that much. Gives me a night off. She's very energetic let's put it that way." he explained in his thick Geordie accent. "Work?" I said, "has she changed jobs?" "No she still works here." He gestured around him.

It was a Thursday evening, and we were propping up the embassy bar. He had pulled a few strings and secured her an admin position in the same building, similar to the role she had in Bucharest.

That's a lot of flying, for a typist, I thought. I looked at him and took a draught of my Boddingtons, on the verge of asking a follow up question.

He seemed to sense it, and at the same time appeared to not want to 'go there', staring fixedly at the bar before him, taking a deep long pull on his beer and looking at his watch.

London. Early 1960s. The city was navigating post-war recovery alongside increasing Cold War tensions. Christine Keeler, a young woman from a modest background, worked as a model and showgirl. Through social connections and the London nightclub scene, she found herself introduced to influential figures within British politics and foreign intelligence. Her striking appearance and charm gave her access to circles usually closed to outsiders, bringing her into contact with senior government officials and foreign diplomats. Christine became involved with two men in particular:

John Profumo, the Secretary of State for War and a senior government minister, and Yevgeny Ivanov, a Soviet naval attaché. What began as personal relationships quickly escalated into a political scandal that raised concerns about national security. Rumours spread through Westminster, and the press covered every detail extensively. Although Christine was not an intelligence agent herself, her connections became channels for information and influence far beyond her intentions. The resulting scandal, known as the Profumo Affair, contributed to the downfall of a government and revealed the complex overlap between personal relationships, power, and political risk.

British spies undergo rigorous training designed to keep them alert to such threats, because in their line of work, a seemingly innocent relationship can be a tool for manipulation.

At MI6 and MI5, recruits face psychological drills, scenario role-plays, and operational security exercises to help them question everything, especially people who seem too perfect. This training often takes place inside the SIS Building at Vauxhall Cross, a prominent London headquarters completed in 1994.

Designed to resemble a crystal ship, the building combines glass, steel, and reinforced concrete, balancing bold visibility with strong security. Inside, advanced facilities support agents in learning to spot subtle signs of manipulation: inconsistent stories, hesitation, or vulnerabilities like loneliness or greed. Experienced officers simulate encounters with potential threats, helping recruits develop emotional discipline and healthy scepticism. Above all, agents are taught to report any suspicions immediately.

Ignoring red flags is never an option.

Sometimes, what appears to be a simple romance is actually a carefully laid trap, an enduring espionage technique known as the honeytrap. No amount of training, however, can fully prepare an agent for the moments when instinct, protocol, and reason fail. Even the most disciplined, impeccably British operative can find himself ensnared, not just caught in a perilous situation, but paralysed by it, unable to act or alert his superiors.

The lines between duty and desire blur, and the cold calculus of espionage gives way to something far more human and uncontrollable. Because, well, tits.

Not long after what was to be our last drink together, my friend was abruptly recalled to the UK.

That in itself was not entirely unusual. To stave off burnout and preserve operational sharpness, the Foreign, Commonwealth & Development Office and the intelligence services generally cap consecutive tours abroad. Usually, after two or three back-to-back postings, an officer returns home for a breath of fresh air, a reset, before the next deployment. He had come to Budapest from South America and had already been living in the city for a couple of years. Yet the swiftness of his recall was out of the ordinary. One day he was there. The next, gone without so much as a goodbye.

Months later, I spotted his Nissan Skyline parked outside a lively expat bar in the castle district. The car that was his trophy, purchased on post with the luxury of shipping it home tax-free. But here it was. At least the new user was enjoying a pint I thought. It's what he would have wanted.

And then there is the final chapter in this strange tale.

Look, I am a professional headhunter. Thirty years in the game and I am damn good at it. I have the skills, the technology and a natural instinct to track anyone, anywhere, that is my craft. Give me a name and I will tell you what they had for breakfast.

But from the moment he disappeared until now, two decades later, not a single pixel of proof has surfaced. Not one digital footprint of my friend or his stunning belle. It is as if they never existed. Nothing. Nada.

Et tu, Fozzie?

So, I started all over again.

I found an office right in the heart of downtown: a serviced space run by Regus. It was perfect. We took a six-person room to begin with, but the deal meant we could expand into bigger suites as we grew. And I fully intended to grow.

I'd persuaded the three Team Leaders from VCI to join me. They were seasoned operators, knew the market inside out, carried with them a ready-made black book of clients, and, most importantly, they knew me. They knew my quirks, my flaws, and the golden rule: If they wanted me after 5pm, they had better have a damn good reason for dragging me out of the Irish bar.

Naturally, I brought Vik too. She was indispensable. The truth was, she ran the business day to day. Lawyers, accountants, payroll, laptops, desks, phones, she handled it all.

If my Beagle once again chewed through the neighbour's fence and started tearing up his roses, it was Vik who jumped in a taxi to round him up. She had a key to my house. When I forgot the PIN to one of my bank cards, it was Vik I called. She was my anchor, my fixer, my safety net.

And grow we did. Within a year, our little band had become 35 consultants strong. We had taken over the largest offices Regus could offer, and we were flying. With five years of market experience behind us, and now backed by a household-name brand, we became an unstoppable force. By the end of that first year, we were the biggest consultancy in Hungary. The Budapest Business Journal even named us the city's number one employer.

Meanwhile, Jon was thriving in Prague. We spoke every day, always for at least a good hour, and he remained one of my closest friends. Which is why the call we both got from Frodo, one dark and bitterly cold December afternoon, hit so hard.

Frodo's title was Head of International. Dream had long been the undisputed number one brand in the UK, and Frodo was part of the reason why. He had joined as a graduate trainee and, with his sharp mind and sharp elbows, had risen fast. Now, five years younger than me, he reported directly to the board and oversaw every overseas office.

But our rapid growth meant he could no longer manage it all. His plan was to split the role, creating a European Director who would take charge of the continent, while he relocated to Australia to build Asia-Pacific. It was a huge opportunity: Lots of travel, a bigger salary, and a step closer to the top table.

Frodo called me first, then Jon. We were both to be interviewed for the role. Only one of us would get it. The other would report to the victor.

I wanted that job badly. And I really, really didn't want Jon to get it. I couldn't report to him, and I knew he felt the same about me.

The interviews were scheduled for the following week. Because of the scale of the role, it would be a panel format. Frodo had brought in a couple of other Big Swinging Dicks from the company to sit alongside him. Each of us would have an hour to present our plan for European domination, in the head office in Victoria, London.

Jon and I both flew in. The night before the interview, we slipped out of the hotel for some long-missed English pub activity. We laughed, drank, and enjoyed each other's company, both knowing that tomorrow would change our dynamic forever. I insisted on buying every round. By closing time, after what must have been at least ten pints, we staggered back to the hotel and into the lift.

When it stopped at Jon's floor, we embraced, wished each other slurred good luck, and he tumbled out, patting his pockets for his key. As the doors slid shut, I pressed the button for the ground floor. I wasn't ready for bed just yet. I went straight to the bar and ordered a large glass of red. After all, I needed something to help me sleep.

Especially after ten pints of non-alcoholic lager.

"To be fair, and to be honest," Frodo said down the line two days later, "you were both fucking shit. You were just a bit less shit than him."

Classic Frodo. That was his version of rolling out the red carpet. What he really meant was: Well done, you daft bastard, your spark came through, you edged him out, and now you're in. You take the West, I'll smash the East, and we'll meet in the middle.

And so the adventure rolled on. First order of business: Visit every country under my watch. Latvia, Lithuania, Estonia, Czech, Slovakia, Romania, Bulgaria, Türkiye, and, to my delight, Ireland.

For a company chaired by a ninety-year-old Englishman, Ireland still counted firmly as 'foreign.' For me, it meant something far more important: A chance, every few months, to smuggle back proper bacon and sausages.

Jon and I stayed firm friends. Sure, the calls dropped off in those first weeks of my reign, him licking his wounds, me unsure how to handle the shift in the dynamic, but eventually we found our rhythm again. When I visited his patch, I still treated him differently from the other country managers. Out of respect, yes, but also out of guilt. I felt sorry for him. Truth be told, if the tables had been turned, I don't think I'd have stayed.

The rest was travel, travel, and more travel. Airports, glossy hotels, loyalty cards piling up points until I was flying first class and checking into presidential suites.

The job itself was honestly, much easier.

With that many countries and that many consultants, you become more figurehead than operator. A role model, not a workhorse. I mean, how much code do you think Zuckerberg still writes? How many boxes does Bezos tape shut? That's the dirty little secret of the corporate ladder: every rung you climb is another step away from the real work.

And I'd grown tired of Hungary.

The endless bureaucracy, the Soviet hangover in every public office, the fucking weather. My new job had me on the road three weeks out of four, and I was grateful for the escape. So the next unexpected call I received from Frodo came as a welcome interruption to the game of Fortnite I was currently engrossed in, and was to change my life.

"Erm… pretty much nothing," I admitted, answering his question: "What do you know about Dubai?"

"Right," he said. "It's fucking hot. We're making no money there, and…everyone else is. So the problem isn't Dubai, it's us."

"How come?" I asked.

Dubai wasn't my patch; It was Asia, so belonged to Frodo. And yet here he was, calling at 4pm, crashing my evening, and my game of Fortnite.

"I don't know, Matt. But it's closer to you than to me. Can you get over there for a couple of days and work your magic? My guess is Shawn" (our Country Manager) "Is a lazy bastard who's gone native, spending more time on the golf course than running the business."

A week later, I was airborne: Malev to Vienna, then Emirates A380 to Dubai. Seven hours and 3 thousand miles later, I descended into a furnace of a city, sliding into a limo thanks to my frequent flyer perks, and whisked to the Holiday Inn across from our office.

The next morning, grateful to escape the three-star fleapit, I stepped out into blistering sunshine, the city shimmering like a mirage, and crossed the road ready to dig into the chaos.

The business was a shambles. Unaware of my arrival, consultants drifted in any time between 10am and midday, dressed in shorts, rumpled, and clearly worse for wear. By day two, they had at least learned enough to pretend they were professional recruitment consultants. By day three, I had ripped through the financials like a forensic accountant.

Hundreds of thousands were vanishing in commissions on fake invoices.

That evening, I was holed up in the hotel's business suite, faxing Frodo key data at midnight. He didn't even trust that the company email's server was not being monitored

It was a real shame. The market was booming, and by rights the office should have been a shining flagship for our international business. Instead, it was deep in the red, haemorrhaging money, and under the very real threat of being shut down altogether. Something had to change, and quickly.

The following day, Frodo laid out his vision to me over the phone.

"How do you fancy moving there for a couple of years?" he asked casually, as if the thought had just come to him.

"Sure!" I replied a little too quickly, agreeing before I had even let the implications sink in.

He went on to outline the deal. My title would be elevated from European Director to Director EMEA, stretching my remit to include the Middle East and Africa. It sounded impressive, a real expansion of my kingdom, I would also need to serve as the Country Manager for Dubai until I could stabilise the business, turn the tide, and eventually backfill the role with a permanent hire. Ideally, Frodo added, I would identify and train one of the existing consultants to step up into the job.

I suspected Frodo had a second motive in play. As European figurehead I had drifted too far away from the coalface, becoming more strategist than practitioner. He had clearly decided that throwing me back into the thick of it, would sharpen my edge again. Truth be told, he was probably right. He was definitely right.

As I mulled it over, I thought back to my journey within Dream: From running a small, outpost in Eastern Europe to suddenly finding myself responsible for half the globe. I couldn't help but think of my mate Jon, who was still plugging away in Prague, increasingly restless and frustrated by the limitations of his role. The professional gap between us was widening, and I worried about the strain it might put on our friendship. I mentioned as much to Frodo.

"Well, that's part two," he replied with a knowing smile in his voice.

Two weeks later I found myself back on the familiar road to Prague, genuinely looking forward to an evening with my old friend. Frodo had outlined his plan for Jon, and I had decided not to hit him with it straight away. Better to enjoy a few hours of R&R together, let the beer flow, share a laugh, and then sit down the following morning to map out the serious stuff.

Meanwhile, back at home, my wife was knee-deep in boxes and tape, orchestrating the mammoth task of packing our lives for the move to the Middle East. The relocation package was generous, another handsome salary hike, full logistical support, even arrangements to fly out our three dogs. The company would put us in a villa for the first three months and line up a local agent to help us find something more permanent.

It was an exhilarating moment for the Foster family. The twins had just turned three, and I relished the thought of raising them in one of the safest countries in the world. On top of that, they would benefit from a first-class private education, all courtesy of my employer's largesse. Again, the stars seemed to be aligning.

I steered my car down the ramp into the underground parking of the Sheraton, the familiar squeak of tyres on polished concrete reminding me that this had become almost a second home. I headed straight for my usual space. By now I was such a regular presence that the hotel reserved me a private bay right next to the lift.

I knew exactly what awaited me beyond the lobby. In the suite, when I slid open the wardrobe door, there would be a bathrobe hanging neatly in place, soft and freshly pressed, my name embroidered across the chest. The hotel had gone to the trouble of having it made for me, a gesture that made each stay feel less like business travel and more like stepping into a private club.

Jon and I had arranged to meet at a small, discreet casino we both favoured, not far from where I was staying. By the time I arrived he was already planted at the poker table, a half-finished complimentary pint sweating quietly beside him.

We embraced. A hug and a few backslaps that carried both warmth a faint awkwardness. I pulled out a chair, slipped into it, and fished my wallet from my inside pocket. Catching the eye of the waitress - an attractive young woman in a skimpy, Hooters-style uniform - I gestured for a beer. The croupier fanned and shuffled the deck, the satisfying slap of the cards on felt signalling the beginning of what I knew would be a long, memorable night.

The following morning we had agreed to meet in a small, traditional coffee shop, tucked away not far from the shopping centre where our office was based. Our conversation needed to remain completely confidential. I didn't even want the Czech team to know I was in town. I had booked myself into the hotel for two nights, but I had no intention of going anywhere near the office that day.

I arrived first, just before ten. The place had the comforting murmur of low conversation, the rich aroma of freshly roasted coffee, and, drifting in from a corner table, a faint thread of cigar smoke. I chose a seat in the rear, a quiet corner with a view of the door, and summoned a waiter to take my order. A moment later the bell above the door jingled and Jon walked in. He looked exactly as I expected: Bleary-eyed, pale, and moving as though the previous night had been a heady cocktail of poker, beer, and a final stumble into our favourite strip club. Which, of course, was precisely what had happened.

He spotted me and gave a curt nod, no smile this time. He looked rough, and I was under no illusions that I looked much better.

I rose as he weaved through the tables and collapsed into the chair opposite. "Morning." He muttered.

"Hi mate. How are you?" I asked.

"Rough. I need a coffee."

"Me too."

As if on cue, a waiter in a starched white apron appeared at our table balancing a tray: Two steaming black coffees, each with a jug of cream, and, more unexpectedly, two shot glasses of a clear liquid. Becherovka. The Czech national spirit. Herby, fiery, and utterly inappropriate for a breakfast meeting.

Jon stared at the glasses in disbelief, his eyes flicking from them to me, trying to gauge whether I was serious. The waiter glided (glid?) away, leaving us to it. I picked one up and gestured for him to do the same.

"Nazdraví," I said, before downing it in a single swallow. The burn clawed its way down my throat and made my eyes water.

"Nazdraví," Jon echoed, grimacing as he followed suit.

We set the glasses down together. The silence stretched. I coughed, blinked hard, and then finally spoke.

"Jon," I said quietly. "I'm really, really sorry, mate. You're fired."

Intermission

The move to Dubai was almost seamless. Within a couple of months we had settled into a large detached villa inside a gated compound. The place was idyllic: A clubhouse with a bar and restaurant, a sparkling pool, a shaded children's play area, and four pristine tennis courts. For my own amusement, I splashed out on a second-hand golf cart so we could zip along the private roads like overgrown kids.

The garage held two cars: a sleek Mercedes SLK 55 AMG, a roaring beast that had once served as the safety car at the Abu Dhabi Grand Prix, and a far more restrained black Mercedes S-Class. Restrained, that is, except for the fact it was literally bulletproof, acquired at a discount from the Philippine embassy once they no longer needed it.

Life quickly settled into a rhythm. Less travel in those first few months as I got to grips with the Dubai operation. In the office by seven, out by three-thirty, then at the clubhouse by four with a handful of new friends. I found I had an extra hour in the day: Jon and I no longer spoke.

That day in the coffee shop had stretched long. The first Becherovka had been followed by many more, each one dulling the sting just enough to carry us forward. We both knew we were grieving, the death of a partnership, of a shared era.

The truth was brutal: After my promotion, Jon had lost his spark. He was still a gifted headhunter, a natural leader whose empathy and instinct carried whole teams on his back like Atlas. But once a star begins to fade, reversing the decline is rarely possible.

His numbers fell, the energy drained, and to make matters worse one of his senior managers, a top biller, had been courted by a rival. He had bypassed Jon and me and made a call straight to Frodo. The offer was for a Country Manager role, and, unless we could match it, he was inclined to go.

I had argued, bargained, begged for time. None of it mattered. The final blow was cold and simple: If I refused, then I would be the one out. And so, with a heavy heart, I dialled my friend and set up that meeting.

With that chapter closed, I buried myself in Dubai. Staff changes, big wins, marquee clients. A member of the Royal Family telling me he wanted me.

Yes, really.

So, pour yourself a strong coffee - or better yet, a generous glass of red - and I'll tell you how it happened.

Mr Ambassador

I pointed the nose of the S Class Mercedes onto the down ramp leading to the office underground car park and childishly gunned the engine slightly too much in order to create a dragon's howl as the V8 monster reverberating around the concrete canyon.

My colleague Andy, in the passenger seat, or rather curled up in the footwell of the passenger seat, was noisily finishing a petrol station hotdog. I was smoking my usual Marlboro Gold, with all the tinted windows closed. The cockpit was filled with a thick carcinogenic fog, which swirled genie-like towards freedom once I had switched off the engine and opened the drivers' door.

We spotted a handful of our colleagues huddled in the shadows of the car park. Two of them were smoking cigarettes, one had a filled baguette concealed beneath his jacket lapel, He bent his head downwards, with his free hand lifted his jacket front to cover his face and presumably took a bite.

The air in the car park was stifling. Outside in the fresh air the temperature was in the high 30s, the humidity levels so high that the instant you left the airconditioned building your sunglasses fogged up as if a switch had been flipped. My colleagues, and rapidly Andy and I, were covered in the Dubai film of sweat which descends upon everybody who dares to step into the open air between the months of April and October.

In a distant corner of the car park stood a small group of Indians, office workers, presumably from the IT consultancy above us. They were spitting profusely around their own feet. I watched them in disgust, until I felt a sharp pain in my fingers. I had forgotten about the cigarette I had hidden up my jacket sleeve, and it had decided to remind me of its presence. The two groups regarded each other, like Poundland versions of the Jets and the Sharks in Middle East Side Story.

I threw down my cigarette and stamped it out.

"Come on, lab rats, let's make some money."

We shuffled towards the stairwell which led away from the parking lot and towards our office. Dubai in Summer can be challenging, punishing even. Dubai in Summer, sporting a woollen pinstripe suit cannot in all good conscience be advised. This particular day also happened to be halfway through the holy period of Ramadan. For a Muslim, a sacred period of self-sacrifice and reflection. For a bunch of non-Muslim expat recruiters, it's a month of smoking, eating and drinking in secret during daylight hours, whether that be in the footwell of an S Class, or the murky shadows of a car park. The only benefit of the four or so weeks for non-believers being that we finished work at 2pm and could therefore get to McGettigan's Irish bar sooner than usual, with the result being by teatime everybody was already nicely smashed. For an expat, Ramadan hails a confusion of feelings ranging from a Dunkirk spirit to a month-long's-worth of snow days.

We filed into the office. It was quiet and half empty; None of our Muslim colleagues came in at all during Ramadan. The fifteen or so remaining consultants looked up as we took our seats, the brown nosers nodding and smiling at me, the underperformers staring viciously and quizzically at their computer screens.

I slumped down into my leather swivel chair as Vicky, whose desk was next to mine, slid me a hot milky coffee. For a long period of my life there was a strong possibility that out of the holy trinity of coffee, cigarettes and beer I would be found at any time with at least two of them at once in my hand.

"Anything fun happened?" I asked.

It was nearing midday. I had been out with Andy on what we called a joint client visit. He wasn't our best biller, by a long way, but I enjoyed his company, and I was in a good mood. Plus, McGettigans opened in two hours.

Vicky consulted a small handful of post it notes.

"Claire asked if she could have ten minutes when you got back."

"OK, I'm not back yet. Anything else?"

"The British Embassy called, the Ambassador wants to speak to you because Sheikh Mahand wants to buy the company."

I turned to Vicky, the coffee cup rim nestling on my bottom lip.

"The who called for what?"

I took the post-it note and quickly scanned the office. Our Dubai office had gained, quite deservedly it must be said, a reputation for being a bunch of sun-loving workshy mavericks. It was the main reason I had been sent here, to kick some productivity into them. However, my work in progress was just that, and I fully expected to see a bunch of giggling layabouts huddled around a mobile phone, expecting me to call it and ask for the British Ambo.

It wasn't to be. A couple of consultants caught my gaze and diligently stared hard at their screens. I looked at the name and number on the post it, then looked back at Vicky. "I am not shitting you." She said.

I wasn't a stranger to diplomatic circles. As a teenager I had applied for the Civil Service fast-stream. It's the only application, interview, promotion or similar procedure I ever failed. In a different world I could have been one of those diplomats. I certainly had the flexible attitude to work and dedication to self-enrichment that most of those who I had met possessed.

Once in Budapest I received a call from a company we had never worked with before. A Turkish ceramic tiling business. They asked to meet me specifically as they had some complicated hiring needs over the next year or so and wanted to work through some budgets and timelines with me.

I met them in the office behind their flagship store. After the obligatory first few minutes of pleasantries my BS detector started a little Irish jig in my brain. The pleasantries seemed to form the lion's share of the agenda. As much as I tried to steer the conversation back to the job at hand, the Turkish CEO and his lackey displayed a much greater interest in me personally, my goals, aspirations, family life, and quite concerningly, my military background.

At some point, the CEO mumbled some nonsense about how my thoughts on his business had been invaluable and that he would certainly ruminate on my wisdom before calling me back at some point in the future. He then went on, matter of factly, to tell me about his cousin, who also found himself to be stationed in Budapest, and who just happened to be the Turkish Military Attache to the country, and he to greatly enjoyed meeting other expats. Maybe he could set up a meeting between myself and his cousin?

Now, hindsight is 2020, and the fact that you are reading about this in a blockbusting record-breaking bestselling memoir would suggest that there was more to - A couple of ex- military strangers from opposite sides of an ideological barrier being invited to enjoy a blind date - than meets the eye. And of course it turned out to be. But at the time, in a city not bursting at the seams with expats, it was always quite refreshing to meet likeminded aliens, who, if not exactly in the same boat, were certainly navigating the same choppy waters. That, and perhaps even if I did suspect a little foul play, my curiosity would lead me to accept and find myself standing outside the Turkish embassy on a side road just off the majestically bestatued Hero's Square one Thursday afternoon.

I rang the bell. A young woman opened the door and greeted me with a brief nod. She motioned me inside and led me through the quiet halls. The walls were lined with polished wood panels and faded tapestries that depicted various long-forgotten military victories. Heavy carpets muffled our footsteps.

We stopped outside a door. She knocked firmly. A voice called, "Enter." She pushed the door open and gestured me inside.

The room was simple and formal. Dark wooden furniture, a large desk cluttered with papers and a laptop, and a flag standing guard in the corner. Behind the desk sat a tall man with sharp features and dark, watchful eyes. His black hair was cropped short, streaked with grey at the temples, and his posture was military straight.

The small talk began as he mentioned how Budapest was getting more expensive. Rent rising, prices climbing, it was the backdrop to every conversation here, a constant reminder of the city's shifting pace.

"My cousin tells me you are a very accomplished businessman, Mr Foster."

"Your cousin is too kind." I countered.

"You have a name in the city as being, how you say, top of your division?"

"Now that I will agree with." I said. I don't know of a more reliable team of headhunters in the region, let alone the city."

He paused and looked me in the eye. A look, which by its stillness, turned into a stare.

"You must mix in very influential circles." He looked down to stir his coffee, before continuing, his eyes fixed on the China cup before him.

"Businessmen, politicians." His eyes rose to meet mine. "Spies."

"It's a small city." I agreed cautiously.

He paused again, before:

"My daughter went to university in Manchester, Mr Foster." I visited her many times. Very rainy. I experienced how the hard-working British relax and unwind. The Pints! Oh so many pints." He paused. "It is good to how do you say, chill out? You take some pints, maybe you loosen your tongue a little? It is all good! Of course, maybe accidentally you spill." He gestured his open hand towards me. "Or learn, a few…secrets?"

Then he leaned forward, hands on the desk, voice lowering. "The fewer secrets there are between countries, the less suspicion. Less suspicion means less chance of conflict." His gaze held mine steady. "When information is hidden, doubts grow. Doubts lead to mistrust. And mistrust leads to problems nobody wants." He added, "It's not about giving everything away. It's about sharing enough to stop the worst assumptions."

He studied me, as if weighing my response. "You're a military man, Mr Foster. You know the kind of information countries think they must keep secret. But really, the more light there is, the less suspicion." He continued.

"Security brings stability. Stability brings prosperity. If you can help my country become more prosperous, then of course, some of that financial success would be shared with those who help make it happen. That's just how things work."

He reached across the desk and slid an envelope toward me. Thick, embossed with the Turkish coat of arms.

"This is an invitation to an ambassador's reception. It would be an honour if you and your good lady, Ilona Varga Foster, could attend."

I looked down and saw my full name and home address clearly printed on the front.

Strange rules, strange rulers

Vicky repeated herself:

"I'm not shitting you." She said. snapping my attention back to the present day and the fact that the British Ambo had been asked by Sheikh Mahand to ask Mr. Matt if he would kindly consider selling him the Dubai portion of one of the world's largest privately owned recruitment firms.

I call him Sheikh Mahand. Clearly that's not his real name. In truth the dignitary in question was actually Sheikh Rattlenroll. Sorry, sorry. This particular Sheikh was, and still is, a very very senior member of the UAE Royal Family. Every other street and square in the Emirate of Abu Dhabi bearing the name of his uncles, great uncles or grandfather. To this day he remains a very close friend of mine, and I have no intention of outing him here.

I dialed the number, and it was quickly answered.

"Hello, British Embassy."

"Er Hi, my name is Matt Foster. I'm returning a call from the Ambassador."

"Hold the line."

I looked at Vicky, who was sitting back in her chair and looking right back at me.

3 days later I am gunning the AMG South on Sheikh Zayed Road, the main artery through the desert dunes joining Dubai and the capital city, Abu Dhabi.

There are no postcodes in the UAE. Instead, a delivery driver, visitor, supplier or client will ask for a 'Landmark'. Such as Villa 128, Al Muntazah, by the Ibn Battuta Mall, or Pizza Hut, Street 42, Abu Dhabi, by the Royal Palace. My destination this Thursday morning was quite simple, The Royal Palace.

The ambassador had explained what little he knew about the situation, he seemed as bemused as I was, but politely and accurately relayed the facts in the manner that diplomats are wont to do.

"I bumped into Sheikh Mahand at the Embassy Iftar a couple of evenings ago." He explained. An iftar being a lavish buffet served every evening during Ramadan at which the devotees break their fast of the day. Sumptuous affairs they are indeed. If you ever get the chance to attend one, please do so. Then let me know how it was, as Iftars, being dry affairs, and what with the pubs being open at the same time, are the kind of events I always managed to swerve with a clumsy yet convincing excuse.

"He told me that he had heard your company has set up in the UAE, and, well, he would like to buy it."

I looked at the digital display. 110 MPH. Now, the following is simply my own, unsolicited opinion and in no way is it meant to serve as an invitation to, or condonation of breaking, nay, obliterating the speed limit should you find yourself in the UAE.

For a start, everyone does it. Powerful cars, petrol being cheaper than water, pristine road surfaces, arrow-straight motorways. It's actually safer than sticking to the prescribed speed limit; Find yourself driving at 80, no matter which lane you are in, and soon you will attract a hungry Landcruiser sniffing your exhaust pipe as if the driver is trying to clamber into your boot.

There are cameras, and fines are issued, by they don't carry the social stigma we flagellate ourselves with here in the UK. Once a year, as you take your car for its MOT equivalent, you pay the fines you have accumulated over the last twelve months. One time, late into my deployment to the country, due to a combination of knowing the exact location of all the cameras and my having a driver take me on longer journeys, I found myself in the unusual position of having no fines to pay during the annual checkup. The official before me squinted at his screen, tapped it with a pen, nudged his neighbour who rolled his chair over, joined in the squinting, tapped the screen harder with a bigger pen, then picked up his phone to call a supervisor.

The supervisor duly arrived with a fucking massive pen - no he didn't - but he did arrive and proceed to question me rather aggressively I thought as to why I had no speeding fines, what had I done to their computer system and just who did I think I was? I felt more like a criminal for having racked up precisely zero infractions than if I had been caught drunk driving with one leg out of the window.

There was a radio advert at the time, on Dubai 92, as the fines system was in the process of going digital. It was designed and paid for by the RTA, the Roads and Transport Authority, and the Dubai Police. It began with a jaunty jingle, followed by a clearly overexcited Indian gentleman explaining breathlessly that if you chose to pay your speeding fines online you would be entered into a prize draw and be in with the chance of winning ipads, iphones or even a 5.2 litre supercharged 700 bhp Ford 150 Raptor R! The more fines you get, the greater the chance of winning!

As you can imagine, car crashes were not an uncommon occurrence. And here we bear witness to another of the UAE's - rather dark in my opinion - eccentricities.

At the scene of a collision, the police will arrive - Invariably in a car much more expensive than both of the offending vehicles combined - and proceed to issue the respective drivers with either a red slip or a green slip. Unsurprisingly, the colours denote who was at fault and who was the victim.

The whole encounter will be very respectfully and civilly carried out, always by ridiculously smartly dressed officers. The stark contrast to the paramilitary yobbos we enjoy in the UK being very apparent, but then again, it's not often you will see a UAE copper rolling around in dog shit outside a Wetherspoons at 10pm wrestling a bottle of WKD from a thirty-year-old topless grandma.

Anyway, back to the dark bit. The decision as to which colour slip is issued, sometimes may bear a passing relation to the facts of the crash, but more often than not, will be associated with the nationality of the individual drivers.

Top of the food chain here are the Emiratis, who compose roughly 10% of the whole population. You have the audacity to be sitting patiently in your car at a red light and have a screaming Emirati bowl into your arse at 50 whilst smoking a shisha, and you are getting a red slip.

At number 2 this week in top of the cops are any other nationality Arabs. Followed by:

3 Caucasians

4 Educated Indians,

5 Philippinos,

And bringing up the rear and owning the dubious honour of always being at fault in a collision, no matter what the fuck actually happened, the blue-collar workers from the sub-continent.

You need a driving licence to drive a car in Dubai. Looking at the state of half of them, driving as if they're trying to put a fire out in the boot, you could be forgiven for thinking this not to be the case, but it's true. The process for a Brit is relatively simple. You take your UK driving licence to the RTA, Have your picture taken, a quick eye test, they swap it for a UAE licence and off you jolly well pop.

One sunny day early in my sojourn, I found myself, newly printed photograph in my sweaty palm, sitting in what appeared to be a temporary building which served as the eye testing block, awaiting my turn. Now here is the thing, the eye test 'poster' is one you have seen time and again. A big, huge letter, followed by an increasingly decreasing in size number of letters, culminating in what appears to be a conga of ants along the bottom of the chart.

In this case it is posted on one wall of the building, with the nervous squinting contestant standing at the opposite wall, roughly fifteen feet away.

However, the chairs forming the waiting area are positioned along the wall which joins the two walls together. I'm dutifully awaiting my turn, on a sweaty plastic chair, swapping my gaze between the current testee to my left and the much larger than life and oh-so-very readable eye test not five feet away from me to my right. Flicking my gaze between the two as if attending an invisible tennis match.

The unfortunate driver to be, who up until sixty seconds ago had been seated even closer to the offending eye chart than I was, appeared to be struggling to pass, and was eventually bundled out of a side door by an offended official, presumably on his way to the bus-pass authority.

I stood up, walked away from the eye chart, turned around, recited the letters I had memorised over the last five minutes, and left to collect my prize, wondering just when the hidden camera would be revealed, I would be accosted by the Gulf version of Ant and Dec and we would all have a jolly old guffaw about the ridiculousness of it all. That didn't happen and I found myself outside, clutching my pass certificate, and blinking at either the relentlessness of the sun or the frankly bizarre experience I had just partaken in.

I'm now in a large one-person office. The pleb's side of a voluminous desk, being served Turkish coffee by an immaculately uniformed waiter, whist the Head of the RTA holds my Her Majesty's driving licence in one hand, a large Cuban cigar in the other hand, and my full attention as he explains the problem.

This part is not normal; I should have been out of here an hour ago and on my way to Al Futtaim motors to reduce their inventory by exactly one Mercedes.

Let me back up a little. Previous to this encounter, I was in a much smaller office, watching a much less important official brandish a rubber stamp temptingly 6 inches above my application as his facial expression evolved from bored via quizzical to finally rest upon 'not a fucking clue', as he lowered the stamp and slid my licence back towards my side of the desk.

'Mr. Matt, I am sorry, your licence has expired."

"What?" I snatched it up, turned it over and proffered it back towards the man.

"It's 2045. Expires in 2045." I helpfully rested my finger under the figures which said 2045 to save him the hard work of reading the whole licence.

"Your licence is good till 2045, but your picture expired last year."

It was true. The photograph must be updated every ten years, to your UK home address. But as I had been living in Hungary for the last ten years, with no UK address, it was not something I had been able to, or frankly even knew I had to do.

"OK fine, so what is the procedure?"

"I don't know."

"You don't know?"

"No."

"Oh."

He gently pushed my licence back toward me and looked over my shoulder as if to summon the next customer.

"So what?" I said, equally gently pushing the licence back toward him. "So, what do we do now?"

"You must go see the head of the RTA."

"And he will be able to approve it or whatever?"

"Insha'Allah."

So now I am confidently sitting opposite the head of the RTA, consuming both his coffee and his cigar smoke and hopeful of a positive and swift outcome. The previous official had clearly said Insha'Allah.' Which means 'God willing'. So not only had he referred me to the head honcho in the department, but he had also told me that he had called upon the powers of God to ensure a successful conclusion to the whole matter. Insha'Allah. Listen Mr. Matt. Not only do I want you to get this licence, but I also firmly believe that the big beardy fellow wants it too so frankly we are cooking with gas here and the whole thing is a slam dunk!

Insha'Allah does not mean, God wills it. It means *If* God wills it. It is an oft-used suffix to display our helplessness to control our destiny should that differ from the predetermined path Allah has chosen for us. When used in a real-time scenario, especially with any official or decision-maker of any kind in the Middle East, its real meaning needs to be interpreted as anywhere from 'If I can be bothered' to 'Not a fucking chance.'

I am ruminating on my naivety as the head of the RTA is explaining how we should tackle the situation. Because I have no driving licence, according to him, I would have to undergo the standard procedure to acquire the licence in such a situation, a minimum of 40 hours of driving lessons followed by a driving test. But also according to him, what with him being the Head of the RTA and dead powerful all that, and me being a clearly nice, wholesome white, British businessman in a very smart suit, and not one of those troublesome workers from the subcontinent, he would waive the driving lessons, fast forward straight to the driving test, which I would pass with flying colours and we could all then reconvene and smoke ourselves silly.

The driving test itself lasted no more than 20 seconds. I kid you not.

It was a couple of days later when I turned up at the test centre. I took a ticket; my number came up and I toddled off to the bay displayed on the screen. Arriving at the car, I was immediately joined by three other men, all Indians, and the examiner, a rather stern looking Arabic gentleman. He consulted a clipboard and barked out a name which obviously rang a bell with one of the Indians, as he stepped forward to be installed into the driving seat whilst the rest of us were ushered into the back seat together.

One by one the Indian men took turns in the driving seat. The first two drove for about 10 minutes each before they were soundly rebuked for their poor driving abilities, had their papers stamped with a red FAIL, and relegated to rejoin me in the back seat. My third companion had only been driving a couple of minutes before the Examiner took the wheel and diverted us to the kerb. The Indian gentleman immediately burst into tears, before opening the car door and hurrying away, never to be seen again.

My turn came. As you are reading this in real time, I want you to try to get a feel for the actual number of seconds the test took. We had pulled over to the side of a deserted wide road in some kind of semi-industrial estate. The examiner asked me to move away from the kerb and drive forward. I started the engine and began driving. Second gear…10 metres…third gear. He turns to me. "Where are you from, Mr. Matt?" Me, whilst keeping my eyes on the road, not falling for any dirty tricks, this is not my first rodeo. "Me? I am from the UK."

Him. "Please pull over and stop the engine." Me thinking, *what, you aren't even allowed to answer a question, what a dirty trick!* I steer the car to the kerb he reaches out to gesture for my papers, takes them and with a flourish, administers the magical signature indicating a pass, then turns to face the dejected testees in the back seat. "See?!" He shouts at them. "THAT is how you drive a car!"

So, where was I? Aha, I'm doing 110 down Sheikh Zayed Road on and pulling over to release an impatient Landcruiser who was in the process of helpfully trying to save my fuel by gently nudging my back bumper and reaching down to dial my office.

"Matt Foster's phone, hello."

"Vicky, it's me."

"'Ello Mr. Foster, 'Ow is Abu Dhabi?"

"It's good. Well, I think so, I'm not there yet. Vicky, what do you call a Sheikh?"

A pause.

"I don't know, what do you call a Sheikh?"

"What? No, it's not a fucking joke, how do you address a Sheikh? like your worship or your honour or what?"

"What about just, Sheikh."

"I don't know, I don't think so, I think that would be like you calling me Mister."

"But you are a Mister."

"I know I am, but that would be like you saying 'Yes Mister' to me. And I know you do, and I let it ride because you are Hungarian, but strictly speaking it should be 'Yes Sir.'"

A longer pause.

"Vicky?"

"You want me to call you Sir?!"

"What? No! I was just saying. Never mind. Can you ask around the office?"

"Erm, OK"

Muffled. "Does anyone want to call Matt, Sir?"

Oh, for fucks sake.

"Vicky, ask them how we address a Sheikh."

The general consensus came back that for your common or garden Sheikh, Sheikh would do, as it literally means Lord or Master and therefore by definition carries with it enough reverence to get the job done. For your more ennobled Sheikhs, Your Excellency, and for this particular Sheikh, what with him being in line to become the next President of the UAE should there occur a particular nasty hot air balloon incident containing three specific individuals, Your Highness.

I pulled through the open gates of the palace. There were no tourists, no police, guards or security of any kind. Crime is very rare in the UAE, violent crime even more so. Moreover, the Royal family is loved by the people. Twice in my tour I bumped into the President, Sheikh Mohammed, in the wild, the first time was as we both browsed CDs in a music shop in the Mall of the Emirates. I remember thinking two things at the time, One, how serene and untroubled he looked out in public, and two, why the fuck was he looking at the prices?

The second time we actually had a brief conversation. Sunday morning in Dubai. I'm working, as we did on a Sunday, and my particular task that day was to pay a visit to the immigration office. We had quite a complicated visa issue with a South African employee of ours, one that couldn't be solved through the usual channels, so a visit to the Head office was required. Experience had taught me to block off the rest of the day in matters such as this. I took a full packet of cigarettes and loaded up on patience and entered the doors into the throng.

You know those scenes on the news when for one reason or another a bunch of flights have had to be cancelled so they send a cub reporter to document the carnage at the local airport? You've got bodies sleeping on the floor, children running around screaming, queues after queues after queues, shuffling and snaking and seemingly static. This was the view which greeted me that morning. It stopped my dead in my tracks by the doorway. Just as I was assessing the maelstrom and wondering where and how to enter it, Sheikh Mohammed appeared beside me.

He gave me a warm smile and a slight bow. "Good morning." He said, gently.

"Erm, good morning your highness. How are you?"

"Good, good thank you, Marsh 'Allah. How can we help you today?"

"I'm just here to sort a couple of visa issues your highness."

He listened to the first part of my reply but then was already turning to one of his entourage, an immaculately dressed military man sporting a tremendous walrus moustache. By the time I had falteringly finished my sentence, the General was gently guiding my elbow away from the party.

"Go, go please." He offered another warm smile, in contrast to the dismissive fluttering of his right hand.

I followed the General as we weaved through the pulsating masses of humanity. I'm the kid in the dressing gown in Raymond Briggs' the Snowman, being led on a magical journey, through a maze of corridors, backstage of the shitshow, until we arrived at a grandiose pair of leather padded double doors. The general knocked, and without waiting for a reply, pushed open the door and ushered me in.

An elderly Emirati gentleman, peered at us over a computer monitor, not a little curious as to the nature of this rude interruption.

"As-Salaam-Alaikum." Proffered the General. 'Peace be upon you', the standard greeting in the region.

"Wa-Alaikum-Salaam." Retorted the Bedouin nonagenarian. 'And peace be upon you too.'

"Alshaykh Muhamad yatamanaa lakum hudur hadha alrajul al'iinjlizii." explained the military man. No idea what that meant but I did catch 'Sheikh Mohammed' and 'Injilizi' the Englishman.

"Naeam" croaked the official. Then to me, with a gesture toward the leather armchair, "Come come please sit."

I tentatively, and I hoped, deferentially edged forward until I was aside the huge armchair, and slid into it.

I explained my business to the gentleman. A South African member of my team was due to renew his visa in the next two days, but he was unable to do so on account of him currently languishing in the Al Aweer jail. If he didn't renew his visa, he would be unable to be released from prison, due to him not having a visa which he would otherwise have enjoyed would he not be currently doing porridge in said jail.

Emirati bureaucracy is riddled with such catch 22s inside the vicious circle of a gordian knot. I once tried to open a company bank account only to be told I needed to produce an office lease agreement, and to obtain an office lease agreement, I needed to pay the first three months' rent, from a company bank account. Not for the first time I found myself in front of a bemused official thinking I can't be the first fucking person to have had this issue!

Over the next 10 or so minutes, the official requested, and I furnished the pertinent details of the case. Finally, he picked up a telephone to his left and had a brief but seemingly non-negotiable conversation with an invisible lacky.

He replaced the handset. "Thank you, Mr. Matt, all is done."

"That's it?"

"That is it." He rose slightly and gestured towards his frankly overly upholstered office doors.

"So, Mr. Botha will get his visa renewed?"

"Yes, visa renewed, yes yes…Insha'Allah."

FUCK!

Effing and Jeffing

I suppose I ought to explain why my colleague was currently acting as the Birdman of Al Aweer instead of spending his days making me money and his nights getting turned down by air hostesses in Barasti beach bar.

He was arrested and sentenced to 7 days pokey for swearing at a cash machine.

Right, Matt, thanks for that, makes perfect sense, you say, let's move on with the story.

Wait, what?

Despite being one of the most liberal states in the GCC (*Gulf Cooperation Council,* like the EU but less hated by people with high blood pressure and football club tattoos on their calves) The UAE is still governed by Sharia law, and swearing in public is a criminal offence. This employee of mine had been out on the town, found himself short of the necessary beer tokens to complete his journey into oblivion and toddled over to an ATM. The machine took an instant dislike to him for whatever reason and pointedly refused to furnish him with either the bank notes he had requested or indeed the debit card he had provided. Duly miffed, our friend unleashed a torrent of abuse at the inanimate teller, and was promptly and it's probably fair to say, rather unfortunately, arrested by the plain clothes plod standing behind him in the queue.

Luckily, as he owned a work visa, he was also able to prove to the Sand Sweeney that he had an alcohol licence, or the 7 days would instead have been at least one month.

I'm not talking about the type of alcohol licence we are familiar with here in the UK, the one which enables Janice Cleavage to serve beers wines and spirits on or off the premises. In the UAE you need an alcohol licence to buy and consume booze.

In pubs they are rarely if ever asked to be shown, but a permit is essential if you wish to buy product from one of the handful of government controlled off licences. They are also another fantastic example of the logic loopholes of the UAE legal system. You see, only by providing a valid resident's visa can you be entitled to an alcohol licence, so every one of the 25 million or so tourists who descend upon the sandpit's fleshpots annually are risking pokey when they purchase a pint.

This story, or rather the Dubai parts of it, were almost never to be written.

3 months I had been in the country. It was a Thursday evening, and I was 2 hours the wrong side of propping up the clubhouse bar with a few close friends. The crowd began to thin, and my thoughts turned to toddling off home. The clubhouse was only a 5-minute walk from home, but it was much more fun to take the golf cart.

Now come on, how cool is it to have a golf cart to drive to the pub in? A little four-seater number, two single seats in the front and a rear facing bench. The twins were three years old at the time, and it made them so happy to ride around with daddy.

Generally they could both fit quite comfortably in the passenger seat, but when that was occupied, they took the rear bench and gripped the bars as hard as they could. One time, as we all returned from the pool after a full days' relaxation, I took a corner a little too quickly and realised what I thought was the start of a minor stroke was Grace squeezing on my left bicep.

"Daddy?"

"yes, sweetheart?"

"Harry fell off."

I hit the brake pedal hard, causing my passenger to slide off the shiny plastic seat and land heavily on her arse.

I turned to see Harry toddling up the road towards us, giggling insanely and nursing his left elbow with his right hand.

"Daddy, I fell off!"

Luckily, or Masha' Allah as they say in these parts, being made of rubber as most little boys are, he was physically fine, but it was to be another tale of Harry and the golf cart which saw me a gnat's whisker from deportation:

I pulled up at the villa and plugged in the golf cart - Given the high cost of electricity and the ridiculously low price of petrol, mile for mile it actually cost me more to run the buggy than the AMG - and climbed the marble staircase leading to the oak double doors, and felt the refreshing slap of frigid air that greeted me upon entering. My wife's permanent scowl was sitting even deeper on her rutted jowls than usual. It was apparent that someone else rather than the usual me had bent her out of shape.

Harry appeared from behind her ample frame, all tomato cheeks and snot and tears. It was an hour past his habitual bedtime, and whatever ailment was keeping him from sleeping was exacerbated by the fact he was now also overtired.

"Come on big man." I swept him into my arms and waltzed him out of the still open door, back towards the golf cart which was to be his lullaby. A couple of laps of the block on my knee and he would be in the arms of Morpheus.

Sure enough, five minutes later as we approached the final corner before our house, he was curled up on my lap, sleeping the sleep of the innocent.

"Ah man, what do you think you are doing?!"

A loud, aggressive American voice from just over my left shoulder.

"Helping my little boy to go to sleep before returning home so I can be glared at by a semi-professional scowler whilst I continue my journey into intoxication and count the hours before I can get back to work and subsequently the pub I have just left."

Is what I should have said.

"Fuck off!" I what I heard myself saying.

I turned the corner and drove the final 10 metres to my gate. I stopped the buggy and turned to see which interloper had dared to question my, admittedly rather questionable, parenting style.

An Emirati gentleman, in an immaculately starched kandura, was pacing purposefully towards me, the three wives who formed his contrail quickening their shuffle to keep pace.

I felt a strong icy hand take a hold of my heart and squeeze viciously. The feeling in my legs ceased to exist. I had just sworn at an Emirati, whilst driving a golf cart with a three-year-old on my lap, whilst pissed. (Me, not the three-year-old)

I was out of here.

A few days in jail would be followed by a swift deportation. My assets would be seized. Both everything I had in the house, as well as all the money in my Emirati account. And I would be fired.

Three hours I stood with him by my gate. Three hours his wives waited patiently whilst he listened as I begged, plead, beseeched him to let the matter drop. Finally after the second hour he seemed to crack a little and embarked upon an endless lecture which seemed to encapsulate everything except the recipe for Yorkshire puddings and how oxbow lakes are formed.

Finally they turned and snaked away. I slunk inside the villa, still shaking. Instead of following the well-worn path in the carpet to the spirits cabinet, I took the two flights of stairs to the rooftop balcony, which afforded a view of the distant gatehouse, the only entry and exit into the guarded compound.

I sat there all night, my view fixed on the red and white barrier, just waiting for a sudden blue and red brilliance to illuminate the adobe covered guards hut and signal the beginning of my end. I gazed upon the black stillness of the pool where my children played gaily in the sunlight and felt sick with guilt that I had let them down. I felt lonely and alone and realised that I was homesick.

The Disneyland we had made our home had become a dark and hostile captor. Eventually, a faint hint of a red dawn over the desert made its leisurely appearance, signalling the end of my surveillance, and as I descended the same stairs towards my front door, I realised I was an arrogant fucker, I had again used my charm and manipulative skills to get myself out of a situation I thoroughly deserved to be in. I didn't like me. Still in the same suit I was wearing the day before, I slid into the luxurious embrace of the car I realised I could soon be saying goodbye to. My adopted country had viciously turned on me. I was scared and miserable and I wanted to go home. I went to work.

Who lives in a house like this?

But anyway, where was I? Ah, yes, pulling into the Sheikh's Palace. 'Palace' may be a little misleading, he lived in a gated compound, not too dissimilar to the one I was used to flying around in my tipsy golf buggy.

I aimed the car towards the largest house in the compound, which acted as the Sheik's private residence. It plonked its gigantic palaceness smack in the centre of the estate, easily as large as the comprehensive school I had attended.

I glided (glid?) the S class to a halt alongside a gleaming black Ferrari, Silenced the V8 monster and sat back to take in my surroundings.

The dozens of villas surrounding the palace served as the homes of his closest family members, aunties, uncles, cousins and younger brothers and sisters.

I was struck by how quite untidy the place was. Children's bikes and scooters appeared to have been flung off some giant buckaroo and left to rust where they fell. A few of the villas sported washing lines adorned with various items of clothing, including a purple spangly G string which earned itself a double take from me. As well as the expected fleet of supercars, there seemed to be an equal amount of battered Toyota pick-ups, as if the Taliban had gate-crashed one of Elton John's parties.

I left the air-conditioned comfort of the car and took off my sunglasses as the heat and humidity of the desert fogged them up instantly.

My instructions were to head to the main entrance, ring the doorbell and wait. I did both. I was on the verge of pressing the button again when I heard a loud click. I tentatively pushed on the large wooden door, and it swung open. I stepped inside and nodded a smile as a tiny Indian gentleman in what can be best described as a waiters' uniform bowed his way towards me.

"Hi, I'm…" I started.

"Yes, please, please." He beckoned me to follow him as he pushed open an even larger pair of doors, to reveal a huge sports hall of a room.

I followed Tattoo as we headed to the furthest corner of the room.

"Please, please." He beckoned, with a large bow and a larger smile as he indicated a well stuffed armchair aside an even weller stuffed throne in the Easten time zone of the room.

"I should sit here?" I enquired.

"Yes, please, sit, sit."

I sat sat, and he nodded his approval at my completion of this first task. He showed me his palm. "Please please, wait, OK?"

"Of course."

He bowed again, then turned and hurried down the centre of the room before disappearing through the double doors. I looked around. The room was gargantuan, again reminiscent of the assembly hall at my alma mater, completely empty apart from dozens and dozens of sofas arranged around the internal perimeter. I half expected to hear the screams of some unfortunate first-year getting bogwashed down the corridor.

The double doors at the far end of the room swung open. I stood and strained to see who was entering. I had seen Sheikh Mahand on TV and various posters around the emirate.

In he strolled, trailed by a second Indian lackey carrying a silver tray. Perched atop it were two glasses and a teapot that could easily pass for Aladdin's lamp.

The Sheikh locked eyes with me and began his leisurely, almost ceremonious trek across the room, like a vicar ambling to his pew.

I returned his stare with a slight smile and a nod. He kept his slow march, grin fixed firmly in place, as if I was some kind of long-lost cousin he was excited to meet after years apart.

Do I stand? Stay seated? I could rise, but he was still about 30 meters away. I half-sat up, preparing for whatever protocol this odd dance demanded.

He continued his glacial approach. Fucking hell, I thought, this is going to take forever. I half expected him to pull out one of those swinging incense burners from under his kandura and start waving it around his head.

I finally fully raised myself from the chair, tugged my jacket taut, and straightened my tie. Then it hit me: Should I be walking towards him? Is he expecting me to meet him halfway?

Still, the grin persisted.

I figured he was close enough to hear me, so I broke the silence with, "Your Highness!" a bit louder than necessary to cover the distance.

Taking a few steps forward, I raised a hand for a handshake.

His grin never faltered. As he drew near, he suddenly threw his arms wide open. Fucking Hell, I thought, he's going to hug me. I spread my arms too and took a couple of paces forward to embrace him,

The lackey discreetly whisked off the Sheikh's outer garment. The Sheikh lowered his arms and sidled up next to me, leaving me standing there with two arms outstretched like a fucking melon. I flushed, dropped my arms, and offered a proper handshake instead, which he took, finally ending the awkward dance.

"Mr Matt. How are you? How are you?"

How does he do that? Talking while keeping the same grin he's worn since his grand entrance.

"I'm good, thanks, Your Highness. Very good. It's a pleasure to meet you."

We were still shaking hands. He held on firmly, studying me like he was trying to figure something out.

"Good. Good." He went on. "And how are you?"

"Erm, yes. I'm good. Your Highness. Thank you."

"Good, good." He beamed, still clutching my hand, still trying to read my mind. Well, there is nothing about this that isn't absolutely fucking awkward, I thought. I started loosening my grip, easing our hands apart, hoping like hell he'd get the hint, and we wouldn't end up holding hands the whole fucking meeting.

Thank God, he finally let go and gestured towards the chair next to the enormous throne I had just vacated. "Please sit, please." he beamed. My eyes drifted to the throne I'd been occupying and then to the much smaller, but still ridiculously plush chair beside it. Oh, great, I'd been sitting in his chair.

"Thank you, Your Highness." I said, sinking into my rightful seat.

He settled beside me. Then, without breaking eye contact, he extended his right hand towards the lackey, who swiftly and silently lifted the teapot from the tray and filled two glasses. Still keeping his focus on me, the Sheikh took a glass, lifted it, and slurped half the contents like a man desperate for caffeine. The lackey moved over to me and offered the second glass. I took it. The drink was hot, sweet, with a hint of spice, and surprisingly good. I couldn't tell if it was tea, coffee, or some weird hybrid.

The Sheikh lowered his glass to his lap. "So, Mr Matt, how are you?"

Oh for fuck's sake.

A wanted man

An hour later I am speeding back up the Sheikh Zayed road, back to the office. My phone rang. It was Vicky. I pressed a button on the steering wheel.

"Hi."

"Mr Foster." Came the cheerful voice of my PA. "How was it like to meet a Sheikh"

"Fucking weird." I said.

"Well?" She continued. "Does he want to buy us?"

I paused and thought for a second, before:

"Yeah."

"And? What are you going to do?"

I paused again.

"I'll have a chat with Frodo, get his thoughts. He'll put it to the board I suppose. No idea." I tailed off as I had just passed an elderly Indian gentleman, on a bicycle, balancing a twenty-foot, on the fucking motorway.

"…like?" I heard.

"Sorry Vic" My mind snapped back to the conversation. "I've just passed someone on a bike carrying a ladder. What did you say?"

"I said what was he like?"

"Erm" I said. "Really nice, yeah."

"OK I'll let you go." Said Vik. She knew me so well, she could sense that I still had not had enough time to process the whole surreal experience, and I was currently preoccupied in arranging all the pieces into something resembling order.

"Yeah sweet" I was approaching the exit I would have taken had I been going home. I did the maths, if I went back to the office now, I would only have an hour or so before leaving again. But if I went home now, I'd feel like a kid playing truant until 4 O'clock rolled around.

"Vik." I said. "I'll see you tomorrow. Anyone asks, I'm still down there."

"OK, enjoy byeee!"

I flicked on the indicator and pointed the car towards the clubhouse bar.

"What, the whole company or just Dubai?"

"Just Dubai, apparently."

It was Frodo who asked me that. I was sitting outside the clubhouse, on a shaded terrace that overlooked the pool. A cold Carlsberg sweated on the cast-iron table in front of me. It wasn't yet four o'clock, so my friends hadn't arrived for our daily catch-up. The pool was alive with preschoolers splashing under the watchful eyes of their mums and nannies. Their laughter, along with the sun winking off the water, did its best to lighten my mood. On the table, my phone lay on loudspeaker.

My boss's voice crackled through the afternoon air.

"What do you reckon?" He asked. I leaned back. "Well, on the one hand, he owns a portfolio of big companies - all of them recruit - so we've got a guaranteed in. On the other hand, he's a Sheikh, which means he can rewrite the rules whenever he feels like it. And then, on the other hand, how exactly do you say no to a Sheikh?"

"That sounds like the start of a joke." came Frodo's tinny laugh through the speaker. "How do you say no to a Sheikh? Very fucking carefully!"

"Exactly," I said. "And if we say no, and someone else says yes, well, he owns a recruitment company, and suddenly they get all the jobs instead of us."

"How much is he offering to pay?" Frodo asked.

"That's the problem." I sighed. "How do you value an underperforming perm-only business?"

Perm-only firms are notoriously slippery to price. A temp agency, at least, has a steady, predictable stream of income. You've got fifty contractors out with clients, each billed at £20 an hour. You pay them £15, pocket the £5 spread. That's £250 an hour, £2,000 a day, £40,000 a month. Nearly half a million a year.

When that kind of business goes up for sale, a buyer can usually justify paying £1.5 to £2 million, knowing they'll recoup in three or four years. But valuation depends on the risks. Are all those contractors tied up in one company? Dangerous. Spread across fifty clients? Much safer - the price ticks up. Is one consultant running the whole show? Risky again - what happens if they get hit by the proverbial bus? Ten consultants? Safer, but more expensive.

You see the dilemma. And that's just in temp, the easy side of the industry. Perm is messier. In perm, there are no rolling contracts. Place a CFO, you make £50k. Fail, you get nothing. You might hit a record quarter, then starve the next. Your "assets" walk out of the office at 5.30 and you just must hope they walk back in tomorrow.

Even if a team of clairvoyant financiers somehow conjures the right number, and the deal gets signed, what then? Your people have just been bought. Million-pound billers traded like cattle. Their inboxes lighting up with fresh poaching attempts from Rec2Rec headhunters. How long before they answer one of those calls?

The buying and selling of recruitment companies is a minefield. And now we were being courted by the sort of man who makes offers you don't refuse. Frodo paused to think. He did that a lot. I leaned back, took a slow pull on my lager, and lit a cigarette I'd just tapped out of its cardboard packet.

At last he spoke. "I'll take it to the next board meeting. Any other business? Oh, yeah, Prince Charming wants to buy the company." I heard him give a wry smile, then he added, "In the meantime, stay close to him. See if you can get a sense of what kind of cash he's talking."

"Sure thing." I said.

"Cool. Anything else?" He said.

"Erm, no. I think that's enough for one day."

"Alright, cool. Don't work too hard."

The pool glittered in the afternoon sun. Tempting. I decided a quick dip was in order before my friends caught up. "I won't." I replied, standing as I drained the last of my beer.

A couple of weeks later Frodo had put the offer to the board, and I was once again barrelling down Sheikh Zayed Road toward Abu Dhabi and the Royal Palace.

When I'd phoned the Sheikh, he'd suggested dinner. I agreed without hesitation. As the miles slipped away, the sea to my right shimmered bronze under a sinking sun, the horizon fading into evening.

I entered by the same doors as before, greeted by the same mini minion. This time, instead of turning left into the cavernous reception hall, we went right, through double doors that opened onto an opulent dining room. I hesitated for a moment, taking in the scene. The table was laid for ten. Nine seats were already filled: The Sheikh at the head, a vacant chair at his side, and the rest occupied by suits of every complexion and accent, a Noah's Ark of nationalities.

The Sheikh rose as I entered, gesturing for his nearest guest to follow. As I walked the length of the table, the others stood too, offering polite smiles and nods as I passed.

"Mr. Matt!" he boomed, arms spread wide. For a split second I froze, wary of another awkward embrace. Luckily, his arms dropped into an extended handshake. I clasped his hand, and we shook warmly. "Your Highness." I said. "It's a real pleasure to meet you again."

"Yes, yes, come sit!" He grinned, then swept his hand across the table. "These are my friends. They wanted to see a real Englishman." He threw back his head and laughed.

The dinner was a graceful affair, touched with the kind of understated opulence that seemed second nature to the Sheikh. My companions, I soon discovered, were all business partners of His Highness. Each had once sat where I sat now, uncertain and on edge, until they - or their Frodos - had uttered that decisive yes. From that moment, the Sheikh became the majority shareholder in their enterprises, and their fates were forever altered.

There was an Italian soft drinks company, its products so familiar you have almost certainly tasted them yourself. An IT services firm, born from the vision of a South African husband and wife, had grown from a modest team of twenty consultants into an empire of over three hundred, thanks in no small measure to the Sheikh's influence and the doors he could open. As they recounted their meteoric rise, my thoughts drifted. Which recruitment firm had sourced such talent in such numbers? And how might that story unfold in the years ahead?

The circle was as eclectic as it was impressive: a Czech arms dealer; a Chinese mother and son whose trade was oil and liquefied natural gas; and, to my surprise, an ex-Wimbledon semi-finalist who had once run a modest tennis coaching business. Modest, that is, before he met the Sheikh. Now his brand carried exclusive contracts with every five-star hotel in Abu Dhabi boasting a tennis court, and he was flying in coaches from across the globe. Advantage, indeed, him.

As the evening deepened, waiters drifted back and forth in a quiet procession, bearing an endless series of dishes from the adjoining kitchen. Fruit juices flowed like wine, conversation swelled and softened like the waves of an orchestra. Then I felt it, a light pressure on my arm. I turned to find the Sheikh leaning closer, his expression curious, his eyes steady.

"So, Mr. Matt." He said softly. "I would like to know. Will Dream become part of our family?"

I set down my knife and fork, swallowing the last morsel of what might have been swan, or perhaps white rhino, and placed the silver neatly upon my plate. "I would love for that to happen, Your Highness."

A smile began to form on his lips. I pressed on. "I would love to. Unfortunately…" I let the word hang, giving him time to catch its weight. "The board feels the timing isn't quite right just yet."

The smile vanished. His face stiffened. His eyes darkened to coal.

"Never say never." I stammered quickly, trying to cushion the blow.

For a moment, he stared at me without expression, as though time itself had been paused. Then, slowly, he returned to motion. With measured calm, he placed the napkin he had been dabbing against his lips onto the table. He rose.

"Come, Mr. Matt." he said, his tone controlled, almost flat. "Walk with me."

"Of course." I squeaked, rising to join him. My gaze swept the table, searching the faces of my new acquaintances for some sign of recognition, some warning. But their conversations flowed on as though nothing had changed.

"Come, come." the Sheikh repeated, and led the way.

We passed through the door, across the marble hall, and out into the cool desert evening. He stopped abruptly, turning to face me. He leaned in, his words low, deliberate.

"I am not worried about Dream, Mr. Matt." he said.

"It is you I want."

Bad news

As a recruiter, I am, unfortunately, well-practiced in delivering bad news. I no longer get knots in my stomach before calling a candidate to tell them they didn't get the job.

I've honed my technique over the years. The golden rule is simple: Be direct, be polite, and as far as possible, be truthful.

There's a certain rhythm to it. First, the greeting. Then, quickly the news. If you can sneak in a tiny compliment about their skills or experience, all the better. It's like throwing a lifeline: "We won't be moving forward with this role, but honestly, your presentation skills were excellent, and I would be happy to stay in touch for future opportunities."

The question of timing you will see hotly debated on forums such as Linkedin between recruiters and weary jobseekers. After seeing a CV for the first time for example, when exactly should a candidate hear the dreaded "no"? Some recruiters reject immediately after reading a CV. Pros: The candidate finds out quickly, can move on, and avoids wasting time on a role that isn't right for them. Cons: It feels harsh. People feel judged before they've even had a chance to speak, to explain gaps, to charm you with their personality or nuanced experience. In other words, it's efficient but slightly brutal.

Some recruiters are so challenged by the whole process that they find themselves from time to time simply ghosting. They just ignore the candidate and hope she will go away quietly. It is by far and away the number one hate for recruiters amongst candidates and one of the reasons we in general can suffer from a bad reputation

And then there's lying. Brutal, unvarnished lying. I once had a client reject someone because they were, to put it mildly, insufferable - a mix of narcissism and poor hygiene. "They just felt you weren't an exact cultural fit," I had to say. Which, technically, was true. It just omitted the part where the candidate's breath could have knocked over a small dog. Brutal honesty rarely flies in these situations, so we dress it in euphemisms.

White lies, of course, are a recruiter's bread-and-butter survival mechanism. "We'll definitely consider you for future opportunities" is code for "Please don't email us again, because you're not getting this role." It's polite, it's hopeful, and it keeps the candidate from turning into a permanent LinkedIn stalker, but it's a lie, nonetheless.

Then there's the "keep warm" instruction. This is where things get deliciously Kafkaesque. A client asks us to keep a candidate on the hook while they decide between multiple options. You spend weeks nurturing the candidate's enthusiasm, feeding them small updates, keeping the flame alive. All the while, they are essentially in limbo, unaware that they are being held in suspension for someone else's decision. It's cruel, it's disingenuous, but it's part of the job.

Giving bad news is a skill you need to master, and it is the worst part of our job. It's about honesty without cruelty, clarity without condescension, and sometimes a touch of humour to remind everyone, me included, that rejection, while painful, is rarely the end of the story.

Every now and then though, there's a call you look forward to. Usually when the candidate has royally screwed up or shown just how spectacularly self-important, they can be. Maybe they ignored every ounce of interview prep you painstakingly put together, and then fluffed the final meeting so badly it could have been a comedy sketch. Or perhaps their general demeanour toward you has been condescending, patronising, and downright obnoxious.

I once had a candidate for a CFO role who, mid-interview, suggested that if he were hired, he and the company should conspire to lie about his starting salary, massively underreporting it to slash my fee. A neat little scheme to save the company a pile of cash at my expense. The Managing Director wasn't exactly thrilled; Apparently, "bent CFOs" were not the droids he was looking for. The MD relayed the news to me, I didn't pull any punches whatsoever on the call that followed.

We also get to relay good news, joyous news, life changing news, and of course when that happens it's wonderful. I have sat in endless interview rooms, hearing people tell me that's why they want to be a recruiter, because they want to change people's lives. Whilst it is a happy by product of what we do, there is only one person's life a skilled and hungry recruiter wants to change. Anyone tells me anything different, I reject them.

"Does he bat for the other side?!" boomed Big John. He, Martin, and I were leaning on the bar in the clubhouse, early evening sun slanting through the windows. Big John and Martin were my two closest friends in the world at that time. Hulking Irishmen with fists of iron and hearts of solid gold.

"No!" I shot back. "He wants me to work for him."

"Doing what?" Martin asked.

I tilted my head back and took a generous swig of the frothing nectar. "Finding other companies for him to buy, " I said. "It's fucking huge. Every company I bring him that signs a deal, we split the first-year profit fifty-fifty."

"Fucking hell." muttered Big John, draining his pint and letting the glass crash against the wooden bar with satisfying finality.

"I'm talking to companies every day who would want in." I added. "We could clean up here."

"What's this 'we' business, Kemosabe?" Big John said, eyes twinkling as he greeted the arrival of a fresh pint.

"I figured we could all do it." I shrugged. "Like a consortium."

"Fuck yeah!" Martin chimed. "Count me in."

"Yeah, why the hell not?" Big John agreed, then froze mid-sip. "We don't have to do any three-hour dinners with no fuckin' booze, do we?" His gaze narrowed on me.

"I'll handle the Sheikh." I said coolly. "You just find the companies."

"Right you are." He said, draining his pint and slapping the bar. "Let's fucking do this."

And so we did it.

The next couple of years passed with me spending just enough on the day job to stay off the firing line, and parading a steady stream of hopeful businesses before the Sheikh. Over time, we became very close, largely due to the sheer amount of time we spent together.

The early meetings were always the most formal: I would sit beside the Sheikh as he wove his charm through construction companies, auditors, architects, arms dealers, hoteliers, even film producers. Each introduction was a performance where he was always the star. And then came the dinners. Long, sumptuous affairs in the Palace, or the city's most opulent hotels.

I came to admire His Highness's relentless drive. He didn't need to amass companies like Monopoly cards, yet he pursued empire-building with tireless intensity. No matter how vast his holdings grew, no matter the size of the company before him, he had a rare gift: making each one feel vital, significant, indispensable.

Slowly, the rewards began to follow. Martin, John, and I started earning serious sums. So much so that when I walked into my local Mashreq Bank to deposit my latest haul, polite eyebrows were raised. When even Dubai banks start asking questions about the origin of your wealth, you know you've crossed into another league entirely.

The car is the star

"Do you like this car, Mr Matt?"

I was the passenger in his brand-new BMW M6 Hamann. A hundred grand's worth of fully tricked-out German muscle. We were blasting up Sheikh Zayed Road - from Abu Dhabi to Dubai - His great-grandfather's namesake highway. He had promised to take me on a tour of his private island, somewhere roughly halfway between the two cities. The sun hung high and unforgiving, the Arabian Gulf sparkling like millions of diamonds on our left, and a vast, empty desert stretching endlessly on our right.

"I want you to have it."

I glanced over at him. He was staring right back at me. Honestly, I would have preferred if he was looking forward, at the road, which was currently vanishing beneath our wheels at about 150 miles per hour.

My brain went into overdrive. Did he just say he wanted me to have the car? Did he want me to drive it? Borrow it? Own it? I decided to play it safe and let my cognitive gears catch up.

"It's a beautiful car, Your Highness. It suits you perfectly."

He kept looking at me as we hurtled down the highway. There is something unsettling, no, terrifying, about being driven by a multibillionaire whose entire philosophy is that when Allah decides it's your time, there is nothing you can do about it.

"I've just bought a Rolls Royce, Mr Matt. Do you like Rolls Royce? It's a British car."

"They are beautiful cars too, Your Highness. Very well engineered."

"It's British, Mr Matt. JUST LIKE YOU!" he bellowed with laughter, breaking eye contact just in time to swerve violently around a petroleum truck we were closing in on at breakneck speed.

We both exhaled deeply and rode in silence for a minute or two.

"Would you like this car, Mr Matt?"

I chose to play dumb one last time until I was sure what he meant.

"Oh yes, Your Highness, one day I would love to have a car like this."

He looked back at me once more. Fucking hell, here we go again.

"I will give you this car, Mr Matt."

Now, here's the thing. How bloody British should you be in a situation like this? The way I was brought up, we're hardwired to politely decline any offer. It's like a reflex. Someone offers you something, you say no thank you. Then they say, no really, I insist. You say, well, I shouldn't, really. They say, please, it's no trouble at all. Then you say, well, if you really don't mind, alright then, that would be wonderful thanks. I shall (treasure it/share it with the kids/enjoy eating it etc).

Then comes the awkward bit, you both nervously laugh, sigh with relief, and feel a tiny burst of pride that you've managed to navigate the etiquette dance without stepping on each other's toes.

But here I was, sitting next to a billionaire sheikh who just told me he was giving me his car, and I had no fucking clue what part of the dance I was meant to be doing. Do I start the polite decline dance, at the risk of his saying, OK well if you change your mind? Do I accept? Is it rude to decline? Is it rude to accept?

"I want you to have this car, Mr Matt. For you, your beautiful wife, and your beautiful children."

Now, I know you're desperate to find out whether I got handed a hundred grand's worth of shiny new toy, but first, let me tell you what happened right after he dropped that bombshell.

We were coming up to some roadworks. It was midday on a quiet weekday, so thankfully the traffic was nowhere near the nightmare it can be. A couple of miles back, the signs had told us to slow down to 80. Now they were shouting 50, but we were still cruising well over 100. Just ahead, the outside lane was blocked off with cones, set up in that familiar gentle diagonal line designed to politely herd drivers into the next lane over.

But the Sheikh? Not even a blink. He steered straight through the first half-dozen cones like they weren't there, gliding into the closed lane as if it had been cleared just for him.

We carried on barrelling down the road, totally unbothered. Now, as you've probably worked out, given I'm writing this after as opposed to before this all happened, we didn't crash in a dramatic fireball. Instead, we enjoyed our private little lane for a few more miles, right up until a large, stationary truck laying down hot tarmac appeared directly ahead of us. That, finally, looked like it might end the fun.

As we approached, the Sheikh simply eased the wheel to the left, sent a few more cones spinning off into the distance, and calmly rejoined the open road like nothing had happened.

"I want you to have this car, Mr Matt. For you, for your beautiful wife, and your beautiful children."

I'd made up my mind. I was ready to accept. My mouth opened to speak.

Your beautiful wife.

Wait. *Your beautiful wife?*

Hold on a second. That's it, isn't it? This is some kind of twisted Indecent Proposal situation. I say yes to the car, and he gets a go on the missus. Maybe right now. Or worse, maybe later, like some gentleman's agreement cooked up by the mafia. I get a hundred grand's worth of German engineering, and in return he cashes in a future shag with my Hungarian beauty.

I turned to face him.

"I would love to have this car, Your Highness. Thank you very much."

Fuck her. Give me the keys.

A couple of weeks later, I found myself on the E101 bus, gliding smoothly toward Abu Dhabi from Dubai. Well, I say "bus", back in the UK, this would be classified as a luxury coach, the kind Premier League footballers take to away games. The windows were tinted near-black, shielding passengers from the unforgiving summer sun, while inside, arctic-level air conditioning, onboard Wi-Fi, and sumptuously cushioned seats promised a swift and comfortable journey. I opened my laptop and dove into next year's budgets, grateful for the quiet, rolling workspace.

Two days earlier, the Sheikh had WhatsApped me.

"Mr Matt, when will you come for your car?"

A few messages pinged back and forth, and we settled on today, two hours from now, to be precise. The plan was straightforward: take the coach to Abu Dhabi, hop in a taxi for the final stretch to his palace, and handle the transfer.

Once there, we'd head to one of the city's RTA Customer Happiness Centres, Yep, that is indeed what they are called, to complete the ownership process. We'd both need our Emirates IDs. The Sheikh would bring the Vehicle Registration Card, and I'd flash my UAE driving licence and the insurance policy I'd purchased online the day before, now safely tucked away in a plastic sleeve in my laptop bag.

Then came the plate question. In Dubai, sellers can either retain the plate for future use or let it go with the vehicle. Since the Sheikh hadn't had the car long enough to splash out on a personalised numberplate, I'd be keeping this one.

Because the Beamer was less than 3 years old it could skip the otherwise necessary RTA vehicle inspection. The final hurdle was to settle any outstanding fines. Now, being the Sheikh, there were bound to be a stack of speeding tickets. And also being the Sheikh, they would be torn up.

The plan was then to fire up the beast and blast back up Sheikh Zayed Road in time for our traditional 4 PM beers at the clubhouse, where I'd ceremoniously invite my mates to admire her beauty, parked like a trophy in the lot.

"It's not here."

A pause.

"It's not here?"

"It's not here."

I'm standing in the Sheikh's private office. I arrived about thirty seconds ago. Knocked, entered, found him at his desk, deep in whatever it is Sheikhs get deep into. He looked genuinely pleased to see me, which was reassuring. The slight flicker of surprise that followed was less so.

I reminded him that we had agreed to head to the RTA together. The transfer of ownership for the M6. It was all arranged.

"It's not here."

"It's not here?"

"It's not here."

"Oh," I said finally, when it was clear it wasn't here. "Maybe I've got my days mixed up."

I fucking hadn't. But I thought that offering him a polite exit was better than backing him into a corner.

Then, because I couldn't help myself.

"Where is it, then?"

"Hassan took it to Dubai. He's running some errands."

Hassan was his right-hand man whose job description amounted to running errands. If I wasn't in his diary, it was probably Hassan who hadn't put me there or had taken me out.

"Would you like to stay for dinner, Mr. Matt? I have meetings this afternoon, but you could do your work from here."

I gave it a few seconds' thought. Five hours at his office didn't sound like a good use of my afternoon. And if I'm honest, I was irritated. Not just at the wasted journey, but at the slow-dawning realization that I wouldn't be tearing up Sheikh Zayed Road in my newly acquired piece of German muscle. And maybe, just a little, at myself, for having believed the fantasy in the first place.

"That's very kind of you, Your Highness, but I should probably not. I'm taking my wife out to dinner at the Burj."

I wasn't. I was meeting the boys at four at the clubhouse, as I did every weekday afternoon. I couldn't even remember the last time I'd taken my wife out.

"Also, I'm not sure how often the buses run back to Dubai, so I should get going."

He nodded, half-distracted, and sank back into his chair. Then paused, head tilted, looking at me with mild curiosity.

"Is your car broken, Mr. Matt? Why do you take the bus?"

"Well, I thought I'd be driving home in the BMW." I said, letting the sentence trail off into a grin. Soft, deferential. Stating a fact, but carefully. I really didn't want it to sound contrary.

He stared at me.

Blank.

Had I pushed too far?

I stretched the smile wider. Held it.

He continued to look.

Then,

"Tell Miss Danny to tell my driver to take you."

Thank fuck for that.

He wasn't offended. Just thinking. Miss Danny, his secretary, was stationed just outside. I'd nodded a cheerful hello to her not two minutes earlier.

"Thank you, Your Highness. That's very kind. I'll do that."

I was already stepping backward toward the door, hand on the handle, halfway out.

"Goodbye, Your Highness."

He was engrossed in his laptop.

I closed the door and left, Beamerless.

Now, don't get me wrong. The Sheikh was, and still is, a very generous man. He knows well that his immense wealth creates a gulf so wide it can seem like he's from another world. One time, as we were strolling through a shopping mall he owned, having demolished a palace to build it, he walked up to a cashpoint and withdrew 20,000 Dirham, around £4000 at the time.

He turned to me and gently placed the thick stack of notes in my hand.

"Thank you, Your Highness." I said, almost reflexively. And then, my curiosity got the better of me. "What's this for?"

"I think I owe it to you, Mr. Matt." He replied.

Now, I must tell you, he and I had started to act as business partners in several other ventures. Not one of which I'll even begin to describe here. Not now, not in the sequel, not even in the Netflix movie that this will inevitably become.

"Thank you, Your Highness." I said again. Maybe he did owe me something. Maybe not. But my refusal to ask any more questions was not because I was particularly keen to pocket an extra four grand. It was because, in that moment, it made him happy. And there was something almost… tender in his desire to give.

It reminded me of when I was a boy, really young, and I would visit my Nannan, my mum's mum, every Sunday. We'd spend a few quiet hours together, and I loved her more than anyone or anything in the world. Not because she used to put 50p in a jar every week for me and my brother, but because, on a state pension, in a rented house, she was the kind of woman who would put 50p in a jar every week for us, without ever being asked.

I grew up. Took my new wife to meet my very aged nan. We sat on the same worn sofa I'd sat on as a little boy, drank the same tea, ate the same biscuits from a Roses chocolate tin. And before we left, to drive the S-Class to the airport, where we'd take our business class seats back to our woodland mansion in Budapest, my nan opened the same highly polished wooden cabinet. She took out my jam jar and, with a smile, emptied the cascade of fifty pence pieces into her skeletal hands, before folding them gently into mine.

I would not have dreamt of saying no to that gesture, her gesture. The one that made her so happy. And years later, as the Sheikh tried to make me happy, it was the same feeling that washed over me. The feeling of receiving something precious, given with care, with love, with the quiet knowledge that it was all about making the other person feel valued.

I'll never forget this one though. We were having lunch at the Emirates Palace Hotel in Abu Dhabi, hosting a mix of Italian real estate developers, Czech arms dealers, and a particularly fragrant Bulgarian TV news anchor, and her equally alluring sister.

Halfway through the meal, the Sheikh stood up and gestured for me to follow. Whether he was oblivious to, or fully aware of, the intrigue this would stir among our guests, I'll never know.

"Mr. Matt." he said, with a glint in his eye, "Do you know we have a gold vending machine in this hotel?"

I did. Everyone did.

"No, Your Highness, that sounds delightful." I replied, falling back on the polished politeness I'd picked up from a childhood spent reading Enid Blyton novels. It was handy when dealing with the Sheikh.

"Come, Mr. Matt." He said, beckoning, as he reached into the fold of his kandura and pulled out a sleek black bank card. "I will buy you some gold."

Now, it's not often a bloke buys another bloke gold, and as we stood before the machine, I felt a strange mix of emotions - nervous excitement, disbelief, and a hint of something else I couldn't quite place. He slid the card into the reader, only to be met with a flashing message: OUT OF (FUCKING, yes, I added that bit) ORDER.

A bus, a taxi and no fucking automobile

The Sheikh and I had agreed I'd collect the car on a Sunday morning, a couple of weeks after my first failed attempt. I'll spare you the déjà vu of the journey: the obligatory trudge to Ibn Battuta Coach Station, the coach, the taxi, the chirpy "Good morning, Miss Danny, " the polite knock, the careful head-pop and there he was again, the Sheikh, exactly where I'd left him, glued to his laptop, possibly unaware that any time had passed at all.

"Good morning, Mr Matt! How are you, how are you?"

"Really good, thanks, Your Highness and you?"

"I'm well, I'm well." He replied, half-rising from his chair and gesturing toward a generously padded seat across the table. "Come, please sit, sit."

I sat. There was a pause. He gave a small smile, the kind used to break bad news gently or to introduce a long anecdote.

"So." he began. "The car. . . is not here."

Of course it wasn't.

"Hassan took it for service. It will be back in two, maybe three days. Inshallah."

I nodded slowly. There didn't seem much else to do.

And then the thought settled. He never really intended to give me the car. Not truly. Not yet. Maybe not ever.

The Sheikh's easy smile, the casual way he mentioned Hassan, Hassan the ever-present wildcard. Hassan who borrowed things without asking. Hassan who always seemed to be quietly bending the rules. Hassan who without a doubt wanted that car for himself. I could almost see him now, smirking behind the scenes, quietly sabotaging every plan that might shift the balance in his favour.

I never got the car. But you guessed that already.

Over the next few weeks, the Sheikh sent me several invitations to come collect it. I politely declined the first couple, citing work commitments, meetings, urgent emails, anything to keep the illusion alive. But soon I realized I needed a more permanent solution to fend off his well-meaning but persistent advances.

So when his latest WhatsApp ping lit up my phone, I crafted my reply with care. "Thanks, Your Highness, your offer is very kind. However, my wife has just surprised me with a Mustang for my birthday."

To drive the point home, I topped it off with a flurry of emojis: cheering, confetti, balloons, a car, and of course, a horse.

I pressed send and stared at the phone. Sent, received, read, typing! I held my breath for a few seconds. I wanted to move on from this dance, and I really didn't want to offend him in any way. PING! The message: "OK Mr Matt. Thank you. I will give it to Hassan."

I fucking knew it.

It wasn't always a swing and a miss though…

It was a balmy Thursday evening in November, somewhere between dinner and bedtime. The temperature was hovering around the mid-twenties, and I was sitting on my balcony, the sandy, salty air blowing the weight of the week away. I was nursing a pretty hefty Pimms, with just the right soupçonage of lemonade. The twinkling lights of Jebel Ali flickered in the distance. And then my phone rang. A Dubai number.

"Hello?"

"Hello, is that Mr Matt?"

"Speaking."

"Good evening, Mr Matt. This is Suresh (Unintelligible) from the Burj Al Arab Hotel. Can I please confirm your home address?"

Nowadays I would probably have answered, "You are whom from the what about the what?" Instead I just said, "Villa 128, Al Muntazah Complex, by the Ibn Battuta Mall." And went back to my Pimms and whatever time-wasting app was keeping my ADHD happy at the time.

Sometime later, the doorbell rang. I waddled down a 3-storey marble staircase, balancing out a couple of litres of Pimms with a fairly tight grip on the handrail and opened the main front door.

If you replace Julia Roberts in Pretty Woman with an immaculately dressed but visibly increasingly sweaty Indian concierge, weighed down with carrier bag upon carrier bag, at the early onset stages of knee-buckle, standing on my doorstep, you can picture the scene. He proceeded to unload himself, bag by bag, like a reverse buckaroo, until I'm looking at a pile easily up to my waist. Each carrier bag displayed the Apple logo, and each bag, of which there much have been twenty, was filled with Apple products. Ipads, phones, watches, laptops, desktops.

He stood there with a large grin, metaphorically holding out a perspiring palm. I didn't have any cash, my previous nanny having relieved me of all burdensome banknotes a few days earlier (Sorry to jump about so much but remind me to tell you about that before we go much further) so I reached into the nearest bag, pulled out what I now believe to be an iPhone and proffered it to him. He took it, bowed, wished me a wonderful evening, and disappeared back into the Bently whence he had came.

It turns out (I can't remember how it turns out exactly as the two litres of Pimms and the 50 grands worth of free hardware seems to have muddled my memory receptors) That my good friend Sheikh MaHand had minced into the Burj Al Arab for a weekend of Debauchery, happened upon the Apple store in the lobby and with a John Inman-like wave of his hand ordered "One of everything for my good friend Mr Matt."

Indian pirates

The villa came with a nanny flat. Picture a granny flat, but instead of your incontinent mother, it housed the hired help. It was a detached structure at the end of the garden, a place where nannies lived in modest, sometimes downright grim conditions. Despite being just a few metres from the main house, it was worlds away from the family's luxury.

Most were thrown together from breeze blocks, floors left as bare concrete, a bathroom wedged into the smallest possible space, and a couple of electrical sockets. There was no kitchen, no sink. The bed was nothing more than a raised concrete slab, like the sort you'd find in a UK police cell, with a mattress laid on top. Some flats had air conditioning. Those that didn't made do with a fan that whirred away, day and night.

For our nanny, at her request, we built a small wooden extension so she could cobble together a basic kitchen. We even sorted her a television and a cable TV box attached to the one in the main house. She quickly became the envy of the compound. Often, when we returned home, we'd spot a cluster of visiting nannies gathered outside, marvelling at her little palace.

The TV boxes came from one of two companies, Du or Etisalat. Both were state-owned. They supplied mobile SIM cards, home phones, and the TV service, and no other telecom providers were permitted in the country. With a captive market and all the nimbleness of a public sector monopoly, the service was predictably shoddy.

The cable box offered a handful of international channels, an abundance of local ones, and an on-demand movie download feature.

One evening I came home to find my wife at the kitchen table, poring over a scatter of paperwork. I picked up one sheet and immediately recognised the Du logo at the top. It was a bill. That in itself wasn't surprising. What caught my attention was that the page was entirely filled with movie titles - thirty or forty of them - apparently downloaded in the last month. I could recall ordering maybe two.

I grabbed another sheet. The same thing. By the time I'd gone through the stack, we had a total of five pages listing over two hundred films. In thirty days. At a cost of more than a thousand pounds.

What the fuck?

Obviously, it was a mistake. In the UK, I would have phoned customer service, had it cleared in five minutes, and gone off to the pub. But here? I knew what lay ahead: endless calls, multiple departments, and a steady chorus of "you need to speak to someone else," And "Inshallah."

Then I noticed something odd. These were all Bollywood films. Every last one. And they had been ordered in the evenings, after office hours - when Janti, our nanny, was alone in her quarters with her TV and Du box.

The timing was strange too. Some titles had been ordered minutes apart. Even if she were hopelessly addicted to Indian cinema, I couldn't fathom the logic of buying films she couldn't possibly watch in real time.

I gathered the papers and headed out through the back door, crossing the garden toward her flat. On the way I rehearsed my tone. I decided it was probably an innocent mistake born of her being a technological moron, and I didn't want to intimidate her.

I knocked on the flimsy wooden door. Janti opened it, smiling uncertainly. I'd never had reason to call on her this way.

Holding the papers in what I hoped was a non-threatening manner, I began, "Hi Janti. I just got this bill, and I think we need to look at how you're using…"

My words trailed off. Behind her, I saw a pile of old-style televisions - the kind you used put ornaments on - stacked four high. Each screen was silently playing a different Bollywood blockbuster. Above them sat the Du box and three other gadgets bristling with flashing lights. Perched on top of one device was a pile of CD players of varying ages. One stood upright, spinning a silver disc in plain view.

I realised I'd been silent far too long for polite conversation.

"I just wanted to check you're using your air conditioning." I said at last. "I just had the aircon bill through and it seems rather low. Just… you know… fine to keep it on, in case you were worried."

"Thank you, sir. Yes, yes, I have it on."

I bet you fucking do, I thought. Mission control here must pump out enough heat to roast a goat.

"Great. Good," I replied, stepping back. "Sorry to bother you. Have a good evening."

"You too, sir." came her cheerful reply as I retreated across the garden.

I needed time to think. Clearly, she had to go, but it had to be on my terms and my timetable. A replacement would need to be found fast. The twins were only four, I was out of the country most of the time, and their mother couldn't cook or clean.

First step: Get the word out. Normally, that was all it took. Whisper to another home help in the compound that you needed a gardener or a nanny, and the next morning there would be a queue of cousins outside your gate, each clutching a CV and a hopeful smile. This time, though, it had to stay quiet. I didn't want Janti catching wind of her impending departure. She was, after all, entrusted with the two most precious possessions in my life, and I couldn't be sure they wouldn't suffer if she found out her days were numbered.

Then there was the legal side. If the police got involved, she would almost certainly be arrested and deported.

And she knew about the bomb buried in my back garden.

Blood everywhere

Back at the villa, I poured myself a generous slug of fig wine and sat at the table to think. For all her stupidity, I didn't want her caught up in the UAE legal system, the punishment would not fit the crime. I took a slow draw on the wine, sweet and strong, letting it slow my mental whirlwind to a manageable breeze.

Self-preservation also factored in. Three large bottles sat on the kitchen island, their contents happily bubbling. If the old bill caught wind of my little moonshine operation, either by dropping by or by a timely tip-off from the soon-to-be-ex nanny, it would not be her on the next Emirates A380 out of here. It would be me.

Expat "crimes" in the UAE occupy a strange grey zone. The religiously frowned-upon activities, unmarried couples cohabiting, drinking without a licence, turning figs from your garden into loopy juice, are often met with a discreet blind eye. A sort of "don't ask, don't tell" arrangement. But find yourself in any dispute with law enforcement for any other reason, and suddenly that blind eye snaps wide open, and the book gets thrown at you with both hands.

They know these things happen. You do not need to be Sherlock Al-Holmes to deduce that the supermarket shelves stacked high with tins of yeast are not there for a nation of overenthusiastic bakers. Most bread in the region is unleavened and would not recognise yeast if it jumped on stage and started playing the banjo.

Here is a fun fact: the word alcohol itself is Arabic. Long before it made anyone tipsy, al-kuḥl, "the kohl," meant a fine mineral powder used as eyeliner. Medieval Arabic speakers extended it to mean anything purified or distilled. Europeans borrowed it, first for powders, then for liquids. By the 18th century, English had decided it meant the boozy bit in your drink. In chemistry today, it covers a whole family of compounds, but at heart, alcohol still means "the essence" only nowadays, the kind of essence that convinces people they can dance.

Meanwhile, in my kitchen, the yeast was doing its own quiet work, gorging on fig sugars and farting out alcohol and CO_2. A beautiful, simple example of Mother Nature at her most generous.

Like many females, Mother Nature demands, and deserves, respect. The alchemy of turning what is, let's be honest, a fairly repulsive fruit into a chilled, ruby glass of wine comes with its perils.

It was a Saturday morning. The night before had been swallowed by one of our friend Swetha's notorious villa parties. Swetha, a beautiful, magnetic Indian with dangerous curves, was the kind of hostess who could lure an entire compound away from competing gatherings. If there were multiple villa parties on the same night, you made damn sure hers was the one you crashed.

I say, "Saturday morning", but in truth it was the early hours. The sky was still ink black. I'd been asleep maybe two hours when my bladder and my throat formed a coalition and staged a midnight coup against my brain. Defeated, I rose. The bladder was attended to first. Then, thirst. I glanced at the AP on my wrist: 3:30 a.m. Mental arithmetic proved difficult through the haze of leftover celebration. Was this too early for coffee, or too late for wine? Water, of course, never entered the conversation. Coffee risked banishing the delicious sleep I'd been enjoying. But wine? Was 3:30 a.m. "morning drinking" or "late-night continuation?" Screw it. I could still hear the muffled bass from Swetha's villa, two streets away. If I were there, I'd still be drinking. Wine it was.

I pushed through the swing door to the kitchen and froze. My heart felt like an icy fist had seized hold.

Blood. Everywhere.

The walls were streaked crimson. The island was so thickly coated that not a glimmer of quartz showed beneath. Pools merged across the marble floor, a gleaming red sea. Broken glass glittered on the counters, the island, the floor.

I staggered back, one hand to my mouth, heartbeat hammering in my ears. Then a thought sliced through the panic. The kitchen was cold, sixteen degrees exactly, my air-con setting. If the glass had been from the window, the room would have been a sauna. Even now, in the predawn hours, the outside temperature was in the low thirties with humidity like soup.

The door swung shut again, hiding the carnage. I eased it open, my right hand curled into a fist, arm drawn back like I might actually take on whatever monster had turned my kitchen into an abattoir.

Then I saw it. The culprit.

A bottle of my red wine had exploded. Not just any bottle either, but a 4.5-litre monster once filled with Bells whisky, the kind that sits behind country pub bars collecting coppers from tips. Normally, secondary fermentation is done in a 5-litre demijohn, the bulbous sort you pick up for pennies at car boot sales. But in the UAE, no such luck. I had improvised with three empty whisky bottles. Two still stood intact, silent sentinels over the remains of their fallen comrade.

I grabbed a mop, minesweeping a path toward them, then stopped. What the fuck was I doing? If one went off now, I'd be more holes than human. I bolted upstairs to a guest room, grabbed two duvets, and returned. I also found a plastic laundry basket and jammed it over my head. Improvised bomb disposal chic.

Back in the kitchen, I wrapped myself in one duvet like makeshift armour and used the other as a shield, approaching the bottles matador-style. I threw the spare duvet over them, then, keeping my 10-tog body armour in place, gathered both up in a careful bundle.

Now what? The plan was evolving on the fly. The kitchen's side door led to the garden. I shuffled through it, burdened with my volatile cargo, and laid them gently on the cool grass.

The stillness of the early hours was beautiful. I considered the likely outcome if one exploded now, the kind of noise that could summon flashing red-and-blue lights I definitely did not need. Then I spotted a spade leaning against the wall.

Twenty, maybe thirty minutes later, I tamped the last of the soil over their grave.

Today, somewhere, in the manicured grounds of a luxury villa in Jebel Ali, three feet below the surface of the planet, lies a bomb. A duvet-wrapped, wine-and-whisky-bottle bomb.

It may have detonated. It may not. The Schrödinger's cat of viticulture.

Iraq and roles

PLACE: THE 'SHERATON' HOTEL IN ERBIL, KURDISTAN, IRAQ.

TIMELINE: SOMEWHERE BETWEEN THE SECOND GULF WAR, AND THE RISE OF ISIS.

Foreign Office advice on travel to that region at that particular time:

Recently changed from *You are joking aren't you, don't even think about it* to *It's your funeral but don't come running to us when you get your legs blown off.*

I was enjoying a cold beer in a relatively sparsely furnished, too brightly lit and uncomfortably quiet environs of the hotel bar. As a Starwood Hotels Group platinum member, (or one of the 'plats' as we called ourselves rather self-aggrandisingly) I had spent more than enough time in too many Sheratons to know that this wasn't actually a real one. Truth is, the hotel had at some point in the distance past been a franchise of the brand, but it had ceased paying the royalties soon after Gulf War 2, presuming correctly that the Iraqi legal system would be a hill on which the soft-skinned Sheraton executive management would not be willing to die.

The 'we' was a delegation of British business leaders, proven and potential investors, and I'm pretty sure at least a couple of spies, invited by the Iraqi administration with the goal of attracting investment to the region. The day up until this point had been a fairly mundane and whitewashed affair, as we were bussed between a series of venues of which the newly installed and excitable government were most proud, and all of which had the faint whiff of fresh paint. The heavily armed guards who accompanied us on every stop were congenial enough, but their very presence did raise questions as to whether this particular region of Iraq would indeed transpire to be the next Dubai that the overly zealous officials were desperate for us to believe.

As often comes to pass on days such as these where you find yourself thrust together with a medley of strangers, I had struck up quite a congenial friendship with a middle-aged impressively bearded Scottish oil executive by the name of Hamish. I quickly learned that he was blessed with the dour, cynical, irreverent sense of humour which I am unfailingly drawn to, and we were both enjoying our third or fourth beer.

The conversation between us was almost solely limited to taking the piss out of the hotel and its staff, our co-delegates and the state of this pissant country in general. I was booked to fly home the following day, whilst he was due to remain a couple more days to attend the trade show whose invitation I was now deeply grateful for having swerved.

A DHL liveried courier appeared in the doorway of the bar. Hamish cocked his head, half raised from the chair and lifted an arm. "Over here, son!" He shouted, adding with a grin and slightly quieter "Ya lanky streak o' camel piss ya!" The delivery boy paused, seemingly frozen with indecision.

"Over here, Saddam, yes it's for me!"

Hamish was awaiting a parcel of promotional materials, leaflets, brochures etc, to bedeck his stand with the following day. The delivery boy's attention was snapped to the gesticulating Highlander. He raised his hand in acknowledgement before swiftly exiting the bar, only to return a few seconds later behind a sack barrow, peering over a tower of boxes.

"Fucking hell how many brochures you got there?" I asked. "You do realise nobody here can read."

"Aye." He said with a wrinkly frown.

The courier hurried away as Hamish, and I studied the pile of boxes he had hastily dumped between us. We both had to stand to open the top box, which Hamish did with his hotel room key. He pulled back the flaps to reveal, what appeared at first glance to be boxes of mobile phones.

"Whit da fock?" Twittered Hamish as he eased one from its casing. He raised his gaze to me, as if to say, 'What do you know about all this?'

"What the fuck?" I helpfully translated.

We lifted a box each and sank into our chairs. I glanced around the room. It was spacious enough and empty enough to provide the required privacy from the three or four other small groups of our compatriots.

"There's no name on the label." Hamish observed. I looked, there wasn't. I turned my attention back to the phone. It was a brand I was unaware of. I pulled out my own phone to commence research whilst Hamish searched the boxes and the delivery chit for clues.

No. That can't be it.

I looked from my screen, back to the phone box, back to my screen, then held them side my side.

"You're not going to believe this."

He looked at me, eyes wide.

"Go on."

"Right". I started. 'These are Virtu Signature S, gold and diamond edition'.

I held out my screen for him to see, he reached for his glasses swinging from his neck on a tartan cord and peered downwards.

"Oh right."

"You see how much they are?"

"No. Where?" His eyes darted around my screen as he pushed his spectacles tighter to his nose.

"Here." I pointed. "55,000 dollars. Each."

"Whit da fock?!"

It's staggering how far we have come with Diversity, Equity and Inclusion. To think that the position of CEO of one of the UK's largest Oil refining companies can be occupied by a man burdened with a vocabulary limited to just three words, bless his foul-mouthed little heart.

The Vertu Signature S is a phone, not designed to compete on megapixels or screen resolution, but to ooze opulence.

Each one is handmade from precious metals, sapphire crystal screens, leather, and in the case of ours, diamonds.

Each phone is assembled by a single technician, who signs their name on a certificate tucked in the box. The keypad is made of ceramic with each key resting on its own jewel bearing, just like a Swiss watch.

If you are thinking of buying one, why not head over to Amazon to check out the reviews first? Don't worry, to save you the trouble I did it for you. At time of writing, there are just two.

Mark E, from the US and A, appears to be a big fan, bestowing the illustrious 5 stars: 'This is the 3rd one I have purchased 2 for my self (sic) and my daughter and I just got one for my 6-year-old grandson and he loves the ruby power button. Everyone should get one for themselves they will not be disappointed.'

Jennifer Raby, also of the United States, appears much less easily pleased, with the concise yet insightful 'Too much expensive.'

Mark E. Presumably the type of person who posts on Facebook that following his 5 am ice bath he is now just off to the gym. Typed whilst throwing rocks at squirrels as his druid has just been killed in Dungeons and Dragons.

"Six boxes, four phones in each box, that's... Jesus, over a million dollars."

The next hour or so we passed in huddled conference. Firstly, could we, should we, take them home with us? Quickly discounted as an option. The security procedures we had endured on arrival at Erbil airport rendered any attempt to smuggle this amount of real estate categorically impossible. Not to mention my arrival at Dubai, and his at Whitdafock International Airport or wherever dafock he was bound.

'Post them!' you may be screaming into your paperback, or blindly into the ether as you listen to this on your audiobook from the comfort of your lounger by a Benidorm swimming pool. We kicked the idea around, but come on, it's 8pm, we are half pissed, in a fake Sheraton in deepest Iraq. In theory it could work, in practice, just no. Both of us were sufficiently experienced in international business to swiftly send this option to room 101.

Dissemble the phones, disseminate the various component parts to the four corners of our respective suitcases, grow fake beards, take away the number you first thought of, this was getting frankly ridiculous.

Discounting both of us consigning our relative families to history and living in Iraq for the rest of our natural lives, which, given the alignment of the person or people who owned these baubles may not be very long at all, we had to concede our ownership of said treasure would be sweet but short.

I took a long draw on my glass, large glass, OK, half pint, of wine; We had long before graduated from the grain to the grape. There was, it transpired, written on the label of the box, the name and address of the sender, and after a quick google search, I had punched the number into my telephone and was staring at Hamish as the ringtone changed into a click and then an "Allo?"

I briefly explained why I was calling. We both strained towards the loudspeaker as a confused gaggle of Arabic voices consulted with one another. Eventually: "You bring in taxi to my villa yes?"

Hamish nodded at me. I cocked my head back. Jump in a taxi, in Iraq, in the dark, in Iraq? With a million quid's worth of kit. In FUCKING IRAQ? Are you the reason they print *do not drink* on bottles of bleach?

An hour later (Maybe two; This Iraqi wine was playing its part), as the bar staff busied themselves with the tasks of closing down the venue for yet another evening, whilst keeping a respectful distance from the two nicely toasted Brits and their cardboard tower, slipped through the doors an anonymous messenger. He gathered up our stash of trinkets, offered a respectful nod, and evaporated into the desert night.

In the beautiful contrast between simply recounting my memoir and being burdened with creating a compelling fictional fantasy, I find myself thankfully absolved from the responsibility of tying up the many loose ends of this particular story with a convenient explanation. Who sent the parcel, for whom and why? I can't tell you. I simply don't know. Undoubtedly, we were that evening cast as walk-on parts in a much wider saga of romance, intrigue, most likely even criminality. This particular short chapter of my life, like life itself is wont to do, just came to an end.

Night of the long knives

As do careers.

I can't remember how the end started. And why I wasn't surprised.

There is no verified scientific evidence for the idea of a "sixth sense". However, what people often interpret as a "sixth sense" is usually a combination of intuition, subconscious pattern recognition, and situational awareness.

Our brains are constantly taking in millions of pieces of information - faces, body language, tone of voice, subtle environmental cues - most of which we don't consciously notice. When we "sense" something is off or predict a situation, it's often our subconscious putting the pieces together before our conscious mind catches up.

And in tense situations, our senses sharpen, hearing becomes more acute, vision picks up movement more readily, and even subtle cues from others register more strongly. This can feel like a preternatural awareness.

Recruitment is stressful, but it had started to feel downright poisonous towards the end. Both Frodo and I sensed something was off. A few days before the infamous night of the long knives, I got a text on my work phone from a number I didn't recognise. It read: *Hi Matt, this is my personal mobile, just in case Richard.*

Ordinarily, a text like that would have made my stomach seize. Instead, I noted it down calmly. Stage one had begun.

The next day came an email from our Group HR Director. We had a warm, relationship - the kind forged by countless hours spent fighting side by side in the trenches. She asked if I would be in Bulgaria the following Monday. She knew I would be; All senior directors submitted their travel plans to our group chat. It wasn't unusual to double-check however, given the chaos of our jobs.

I confirmed I would be, looking forward to a few enjoyable days with Marin, our Country Manager. I liked Marin. Our relationship wasn't the usual employer-employee rigmarole - He was unique, running his own company under our brand through a franchise arrangement. He paid us a royalty each month, got access to our marketing and finance support, and, of course, enjoyed the honour of having me as his mentor.

Marin had other ventures beyond recruitment. One of our shared passions was winemaking, though his operation was a little more ambitious than my backyard dabbling.

I remember one Christmas thinking I was being clever: Ordering cases of his latest vintage for our consultants to send to their top clients across Europe. By January, many cases had returned, either politely refused by corporate policies - Exxon Mobil being the standout - or simply repackaged and sent back. More for us, I thought, as I uncorked a bottle one evening in the Budapest office.

I poured myself a generous glass, closed the laptop on the day's shenanigans, and sat back. One mouthful and I spat it out in horror. I drink most things, but this was something else entirely: a petroleum-like spirit with hints of horse shit. It was fucking vile.

She replied far too quickly. Would it be OK if I didn't? And be in Dubai instead. Stage two. I didn't ask why - I think I already knew, and I didn't want to hear it. Could be anything: maybe we'd decided to terminate the Bulgarian franchise, maybe a company-wide announcement was looming, maybe they were reviewing travel expenses, or maybe they'd organised a troupe of dancers to leap out of a fucking cake for me.

Stage three: a text from Frodo. Had I heard from HR?

Yes. So had he. They'd asked him to stay in Australia next week instead of touring our Hong Kong and Singapore offices.

Monday arrived. I got into the office early, just settling behind my desk with a coffee from the ridiculously expensive Italian machine I'd had installed, when the phone rang. It was her - the HR Director.

"Hi, Matt." I could practically taste the tension in her strangled tone. "Hi… all OK?" My own voice came out strained. "Matt, I'm in the Holiday Inn. Would you mind popping down?"

No more pretence. I glanced at the few early arrivals in the office. Tell them the truth? That the Group HR Director had flown 5,000 miles to show up unannounced in my own backyard? Just walk out? Invent a story? Fuck them. Not my problem any more. I just walked out.

So there I am, sitting in a meeting room in the Holiday Inn. She had met me in the reception and led me wordlessly through a cheap looking door. Opposite me is the group CEO, hidden behind an uncomfortably large stack of files, my name printed upside down on every one of them. Next to him is the HR Director. As I said, we'd always got on well, but now she's blinking back tears, trying to stay corporate while her mascara begins its slow descent. She looked like every 1970s mining village kid being told, "If you don't stop crying, I'll give you something to cry about."

"I think you can guess why we're here?" He began.

So that's it? Straight into it? I looked him directly in the eye. Of course I could guess. I'd been on the other side of the table too many times to miss the signs. I won't name him, he was just doing what needed to be done. Elbows sharpened, climbing the greasy pole, surviving by making sure others didn't.

Turns out the company owner had decided two CEOs was one too many. One of the two existing CEOs, my boss, was at that very moment having his own quiet execution in an office in Sydney. I was collateral damage in a full DNA purge, a regime change designed to clear the way for this guy to leave his mark.

Like I said, I won't name him. I've done the same thing myself. Maybe not like this, but still. For the sake of this story, let's just call him Bloated Cowardly Cocksucker.

I honestly can't recall much of the actual conversation. I started to go numb. Shaky. My brain already sprinting through impossible calculations. How would I explain this to my five-year-old twins, who thought I sat somewhere between superhero, minor god, and Peppa Pig? Could I offload the AMG for more than the loan? How long could we keep Janice on before she and I had our own uncomfortable talk? And why do 24-hour shops in Dubai even have locks on the doors? Even back then in the most testing of circumstances my ADHD would pop up and remind me that I have been focussing on one particular thing for far too long now.

I remember thinking, You two stayed in the Holiday Inn last night. I couldn't help the small, inward smile at the thought. Me? I wouldn't be seen dead in a place like that. My relentless travel had earned me Platinum status in my preferred hotel chain, every check-in a guaranteed upgrade to the best suite they had. Meanwhile, these two corporate brown-nosers were slumming it in a three-star dump, and I savoured the quiet superiority of it.

That's when BCC said, "Legally we owe you twelve months' salary. But I'll give you three. If you want the rest, you'll have to sue us." That part I remember with perfect clarity. Crystal sharp. I'd sat across from maybe fifty people, axe in hand, some guilty of fraud, some just plain useless, and one who once flashed her nipples at the Regional Director of a German car manufacturer in a client meeting. But I was always human. It always hurt me more than it hurt them. That part of the job I truly hated.

But this guy, it was the way he did it. The smugness, the obvious delight. A man so wrapped up in his own career progression he didn't care who he stepped on. I remember looking at him and feeling a surprising wave of pity. For his wife, his kids, his so-called friends.

Because one day, he'd be sitting where I was. And there'd be no one crying for him.

Areola non-grata

Yes, I know. We breezed past the nipple incident. I've got a few minutes if you're interested.

Back to Budapest. Early days. The business is growing faster than we can handle, orders piling up, and I need recruiters, fast. It's the early 2000s in the Wild East, and seasoned headhunters are scarce.

A personal contact recommends someone. Agi. Young, full of energy, selling ad space for a local paper. No recruitment experience to speak of, but bags of enthusiasm. And honestly, back then, enthusiasm could carry you a long way.

I didn't have time to interview her properly. A major automotive giant was shifting its Shared Service Centre from Munich to Budapest, and we'd landed the full contract to staff it. Big job. Worth a couple of million euros. When it was done, it would buy me that swanky apartment on Zoltán Utca I'd been eyeing for months. Delivery was everything. Failure wasn't on the menu.

I spoke to Agi over the phone. Her English was flawless. She moonlighted as a presenter on BBRZ, the local English-language radio station. Even down the phoneline, her energy was attractive. She was a ball of positivity and ambition. Exactly what I needed.

It was a Monday morning, early June. Not yet 9 a.m. and Budapest was already warming up. The city was baking, and inside my office was buzzing. Twenty recruiters, already well into their day. Two were in the kitchen making industrial-strength coffee, another pair holed up in the meeting room tearing apart our ad strategy for the car company. The rest were hammering phones, chasing accountants, sales reps, logistics experts, anyone the client needed before the shutters came down in Munich.

From my desk, I saw the main door swing open. In walked Agi, dressed, just about.

Sure, it was hot, but her shorts were so short they looked like they were trying to crawl up inside her arse. Her top, a pink bikini number, was doing a heroic job of containing her tremendous cleavage, and the knee-high boots added a final theatrical flourish. It was part beachwear, part burlesque, part pantomime.

She made her way to reception and introduced herself to Vicky. They exchanged a few words. They both glanced over, and Vic gave me a look. One that said, *Alright, Fozzy, can't wait to see how you deal with this one.*

Fuck that. Why have a dog and bark yourself?

I opened my laptop and fired off an email.

To: Vic
From: Matt
Subject: Vic, sort it out please!

Formal dress in the office. Thanks.

Despite the outfit, she smashed her first day. By the time the call stats came in, she was already top ten percent. My gut had been right again.

Later that evening, alone in the square with a cold beer sweating in my hand, I toasted myself for spotting a diamond. With a cracking arse, it had to be said. I drained the glass, smiled, and walked home.

The next day, I rolled in late. Home hadn't seemed that attractive the night before, so I'd ended up at the British Embassy bar with a few mates, drinking like we were still in sixth form. My morning ritual had been slower than usual, and as I turned the keys in the Audi, a burp rose up that reeked of stale booze. I genuinely wondered if I was still over the limit.

By the time I ambled into the office, Agi was already at her desk. Headset on, blonde curls bouncing, eyes locked on her screen. And she was wearing a full-length, maroon, crushed velvet, fucking ballgown! It reminded me of the curtains we used to have in the Odeon in Rotherham where my dad took me to watch Star Wars.

I stopped dead.

Formal dress, Vic had told her. And to be fair, she had absolutely nailed the brief. It was formal. And it was a dress.

My brain flashed back to my first proper client meeting, when Jon had sent me out for a sharp suit, then thrown me headfirst into Buckingham Palace. Trial by fire. And now, I had another important meeting coming up. Tomorrow, actually. The top brass from the German client were flying in for a breakfast meeting at the Intercontinental. It was a big one. Progress report, face time, all the trimmings. I'd already earmarked it as Agi's Prince Charles moment.

But first, I had to sort out her bloody wardrobe.

I ducked into a quiet corner of the office and rang my wife.

20's Embassy

I realise I mentioned the British Embassy bar, I think it's worth recounting here a brief history of the magnificent building it hides in, as well as a typical evening in its bosom.

Back in the early 2000s, if you wanted to find the British Embassy in Budapest, you didn't head for some bland government bunker in the hills. No, you went straight into the heart of downtown Pest, to Harmincad utca 6. Just a stone's throw from Vörösmarty Tér and a stumble from the Danube, A grand Austro-Hungarian building with a colourful history.

Built in 1914 as the HQ of Hazai Bank, architect Károly Reiner designed it in full fin-de-siècle grandeur, vaulted ceilings, marbled halls and warm cigar smoke-soaked oak panelling.

Fast forward to World War II, and Budapest was coming apart at the seams. The city, once full of music, café chatter, and quiet elegance, had fallen under the jackboot. Nazi troops marched in, welcomed by the homegrown fascists of the Arrow Cross, whose cruelty often outpaced even their masters.

The streets turned cold overnight. Deportations began with brutal efficiency. Jewish families were dragged from their homes and were herded into makeshift ghettos, their lives reduced to numbers on lists, their belongings looted, their future lineage erased.

Many were crammed into cattle cars, locked in darkness for days without food or water, bound for Auschwitz, where few would ever leave. Others didn't even make it that far. Along the banks of the river, people were shot in pairs, their bodies kicked into the water. The blue Danube turned red.

Into this chaos stepped a young Swedish diplomat by the name of Raoul Wallenberg. He arrived in Budapest with a fake consular briefcase and a plan to save as many lives as possible, by whatever means necessary.

Wallenberg wasn't interested in diplomatic niceties. He turned bureaucracy into a weapon. He printed up thousands of Schutz-Pässe, protective passports marked with Sweden's crest. He secretly distributed them among the city's Jewish community, some of them being able therefore to bluff their way through fascist roadblocks and escape the torture.

But it wasn't just paperwork. Wallenberg took over entire buildings and slapped Swedish flags on them, declaring them protected territory. Harmincad utca 6 became one of these so-called "safe houses." Technically Swedish soil, though no one really believed that would stop a determined SS officer. Still, it worked. Hundreds, possibly thousands, hid behind those walls while the rest of the city burned around them.

And while the Arrow Cross prowled the streets, dragging people into black cars and tossing bodies into the Danube, Wallenberg kept going, risking certain torture and death should his plan be discovered

But of course, Budapest was just one front in a much bigger game. When the Soviets rolled in during January 1945, you'd think Wallenberg would be hailed as a hero. He wasn't. He was picked up by the NKVD, the Soviet Union's secret police and internal security agency, accused of spying, and vanished into the black hole of the Gulag. No trial. No explanation. Never seen again.

And here's the thing: No one can explain why. Some say he saw too much. Some say the Soviets didn't like a Western agent playing God on their turf. Others claim he had ties to intelligence networks far above his pay grade. What we know is this, he was dragged into Soviet custody, and then he was no more.

Today, there's a modest plaque outside Harmincad utca 6 with his name on it. People walk past it on their way to get coffee or buy tacky souvenirs on Váci utca.

After the war, the building was left in ruins. Budapest had been flattened, and this old girl had taken her fair share of punches. Then in 1947, as the Iron Curtain was being drawn tight, the British moved in. Not tourists. Diplomats. Officially it was a legation, then later an embassy, but it always felt like the kind of place where MI6 might have had a quiet corner office with soundproof walls and a whisky stash.

Inside, you'd find a British Council library, cultural events and film screenings. All very respectable. But this was Cold War Budapest. Nothing was just what it seemed. Hungarian state security kept a close eye, and the place had more bugs than a cheap motel. Still, it was a kind of beacon. A colourful patch of tweed and gin in the middle of communist grey.

In the early 1990s, with Hungary finally shaking off the Soviet hangover, the Brits signed a new lease and threw serious money at the place. Restoration work began. The banking hall was polished up and unveiled by none other than Queen Elizabeth II in 1993.

Every Thursday evening, the Embassy would quietly crack open a hidden door, tucked discreetly into one of the building's weathered stone folds. Behind it, a bored security guard leafed through a battered paperback, seated beside an equally battered metal detector which was well overdue for an upgrade.

Step through, and you were in. Not in as in officially recognised, diplomatic credentials and all that. More like in the way an old-school club lets you through the door because you know the right people or used to do the right kind of work. The kind of in reserved for ex-military, off-duty spooks, and senior British expats. I ticked all three of the boxes.

Down a flight of stairs and past a blank corridor, the air grew cooler and thicker. Then, there it was: the Embassy bar. An underground sanctuary with low ceilings and yellowing walls.

Officially, it was for Embassy staff only. Unofficially, anyone with the right accent, the right clearance, or just the right look of hungover authority could find themselves inside. British expats of a certain rank, their long-suffering spouses, and a revolving cast of diplomats, attachés, and the occasional anonymous silhouette made up the crowd.

They gathered every week to drink deeply and flirt shamelessly with the Hungarian admin staff of the building. Pint by pint, they drained Her Majesty's stash of subsidised Boddingtons.

It was there I met Sam.

Not his real name. We met him earlier on at the Burn's night supper. You know him as Spiderman.

Now, most of the names in this book have been changed, mainly to protect, well me, let's be honest. But this one has absolutely, definitely, 100 percent been changed. Swear-on-a-Bible changed. In fact, it'll probably keep changing throughout the story. Just in case he, or I, get an unexpected knock on the door from the Foreign Office some rainy Tuesday night.

Because, as we've already discussed by now, Steve was a spy.

Didn't say that on his business card, obviously. His actual title was something vague like Second Technical Officer. Based in Budapest, his job, involved touring British embassies across Eastern Europe, sweeping for clandestine listening devices which had a nasty habit of turning up in walls, lamps, smoke detectors, you name it, and just as quickly reappearing weeks, sometimes days, after he'd moved on.

He may also, possibly, maybe, have had something to do with similar gadgets quietly showing up inside the embassies of countries we didn't send Christmas cards to. I couldn't possibly say.

Stuart and I became close. He was a small, unassuming bloke with thick bottle-bottom glasses and a shock of ginger hair that looked like it had lost a fight with a balloon. He didn't look like a spy, but I suppose that's quite a critical part of the job description. Turning up in an Aston Martin and a dinner jacket might work in the movies, but in real life it tends to get you followed, arrested, or the star of an obituary.

That said, he did have a bloody nice car.

Diplomats, the jammy bastards, were entitled to import any vehicle tax free while on post. And Stefan, being single, childless, and therefore cash-rich, went all in. He got himself a Nissan Skyline Convertible.

One sunny Saturday morning, as I was finishing getting ready for an all-day pub crawl with Shane, I heard the low, throaty growl of a V8 rising up from beneath my balcony. I threw open the doors and leaned over the railing.

There he was, down on the street, perched on a cushion in the driver's seat of the Nissan. I did mention he was on the short side.

"On my way," I called, grabbing my wallet and cigarettes before heading for the lift.

I reached the car door. The wrong one. The Skyline, having been imported straight from Japan where they (quite rightly, if you ask me) drive on the left, had its driver's seat tucked away on what we were used to in Hungary as the passenger side. I circled the rear like a man who definitely knew this already and slid into the correct seat.

That's when I saw it.

Nestled in the footwell, not quite in full daylight view, but unmistakably visible, was an object. A tool. About a foot long. Metallic. Homemade, by the look of it. The welds were rough, it was unpainted. One end featured a handle with finger holes like a set of brass knuckles. The other end flared out into a set of three quite sharp looking serrated claws.

I swallowed. Nudging it gently with my flip flop, pushing it deeper into the footwell. I had no idea what the consequences might be if Silas realised, he'd accidentally left a piece of 'enhanced interrogation' hardware rolling around in full view. And I had absolutely no desire to find out.

We'd spent the day exploring the more obscure watering holes tucked into the folds of the Buda Hills, growing steadily more cheerful with each stop. By the time the sun began its slow descent behind the hills of Óbuda, we were heading for our final destination: a tucked-away bistro nestled inside the gated bubble of the Petneházy Country Club. As we rolled up to the security barrier, the Nissan gave a low, satisfied growl.

Then I saw him.

A man dressed head to toe in black stepped out from behind what looked like a security hut. He'd clearly clocked our arrival and was now striding directly toward the car.

Now, we were roughly eight pints deep at this point, so the world had taken on a slightly syrupy pace. I didn't immediately register anything odd until Seamus leaned forward and gave me a look that cut through the fog.

"Mate." he said, low and deliberate. "On the floor. By your feet. There's a… tool. Pass it to me, yeah?"

I glanced down. Of course. The object. I hesitated.

"Quick." He urged. The man in black was nearly at my window.

I reached down and grabbed the thing, bumping my head hard on the dash as I straightened up. Cold, heavy, brutal looking. I passed it to Samantha, who took it with his left hand while pressing a button with his right. My window began to hum downward.

The man picked up speed, now jogging directly toward us. I braced myself.

And then, with the practiced grace of a man who'd clearly done this a few dozen times, Sharon quickly launched himself across me, dug his elbow into my ribs, and jabbed the tool clean through my window.

With surgical precision, he used the pincer end to pluck a cardboard parking pass from the dispenser on the other side of the barrier.

"Beat you, Ákos!" he shouted to the grinning security guard, who gave us a mock salute as the barrier lifted.

"Fucking right-hand drive cars." Sunday muttered, tossing the tool into the back seat. "Had to build that thing just so I can reach the bloody tickets."

Diplomatic brag

It turns out I needn't have worried about my friend's safety, since the world of espionage rarely strays into the homicidal. Everyone knows spies are out there, but the funny part is most governments already know who half of them are. It's like having a nosy neighbour - you see them peeking through the curtains, but instead of calling them out you just wave and keep mowing the lawn. Sometimes countries let the spies keep "spying" just to see what they'll bungle into next, or to slip them a little nonsense on purpose. It's less James Bond and more like an international game of hide-and-seek where everyone can see the other players, but they all politely pretend not to.

One evening propping up the embassy bar he told me a story which illustrates this perfectly.

He was on one of his transcontinental jaunts, this time to Tirana, Albania's capital. The British Embassy sat on Rruga Skënderbeg, named after the 15th-century hero Gjergj Kastrioti Skënderbeg, who fought the Ottomans and, less famously, outlawed telephone tables and prohibited footstools. Hence the name Albania: literally, *the country that likes to ban things.*

He was staying at the Radisson Hotel, just a short walk across the Great Park to the embassy. On the evening of his arrival, he collected his room key - the old-fashioned metal type attached to a heavy iron ball - went up to his room, dumped his suitcase on its allotted stand, and hurried off to spend the evening sampling the local bars and waitresses on Her Majesty's expenses.

After a few hours of frivolity, he lurched through the darkness, back toward the warmth of his lodgings. But the moment he opened the door, his stomach dropped. His suitcase was no longer obediently resting on its stand - it had migrated to the double bed, lid flung wide across the duvet.

Every item was laid out with surgical precision: Clothes, shoes, toiletries, and most dangerously, his gadgets. Those little tools of the trade he'd smuggled in under the protective cloak of a diplomatic bag.

The message was chillingly clear: We know who you are. We know why you're here. We know what you brought. And yes, we can slip into your room unseen, whenever we please.

He repacked his things with hastily and left the hotel to cross once more the Grand Park under the night stars and arrived at the Embassy. That night, he claimed the sofa in the travel visa waiting room as his bed. It smelled, he reported, of Albanian farts.

The concept of the diplomatic bag is older than you might think. Ancient emissaries were granted safe passage to carry their kings' letters, and the bag, or box, or scroll case, was considered untouchable even then. The principle was revived after the Napoleonic Wars, when the Congress of Vienna in 1815 began sketching out rules for modern diplomacy.

By 1928, the Havana Convention formally recognized the need to protect diplomatic couriers and their dispatches. But the true milestone came with the Vienna Convention on Diplomatic Relations in 1961, which spelled it out in black and white: a diplomatic bag, if properly sealed and marked, may never be opened or peeked into. It could be a satchel, a suitcase, or a large wooden crate with the nuclear emblem sprayed on the side, but so long as it bore the correct seal, it passed through borders as sacred and untouchable.

In 1979, I was an eight-year-old boy playing with Action Men and plastic guns. At the very same time, our new friends the Albanians were playing games on a much larger scale, except their guns were real and they were shipping them into London disguised as diplomatic bags.

British customs officers eyed the oversized crates with suspicion, but there was a problem: Under the Vienna Convention, once a container is marked as a diplomatic bag, it's untouchable.

Of course, Britain knew exactly what was inside. How? Because, well, spies. We knew damn well the crates were full of weapons. But when the Foreign Office lodged its protest, the Albanians just leaned back and asked "What, you didn't open the crates, so how do you know what's inside?"

And that was that. Stalemate. The crates were duly delivered, and a few "diplomats" were expelled on both sides. Everyone knew exactly what had been shipped, yet no one could say a word. The British grumbled politely as we do, and made frantic notes in folders marked Top Secret, the details of which, after the fifty-year embargo which covers such incidences has expired, we will be able to read about in 2029.

My favourite diplomatic bag true story ever involved Nigeria and a man who had clearly overestimated his government's patience: Following a military coup in December 1983. The new regime, led by Major-General Muhammadu Buhari, accused former minister Umaru Dikko of embezzling significant sums from national oil revenues.

In 1984, Dikko fled to London, seeking refuge from the charges and the political turmoil. While in exile, he became a vocal critic of the Buhari administration, further straining relations between him and the Nigerian government. Determined to bring him back, the Nigerian authorities hatched a plan that was audacious, illegal, and absurd in equal measure. In 1984, Dikko was sedated orally by operatives who had posed as medical staff, arriving at his London residence with the polite efficiency of visiting doctors. They brought syrups, tablets, and concoctions carefully concealed in unmarked bottles, all presented under the guise of routine "check-ups" or "treatment for stress."

Dikko, unsuspecting and trusting - or perhaps simply too polite to refuse - ingested the sedative, which worked quickly, leaving him drowsy, disoriented, and easy to handle. By the time the operatives were finished, he was unconscious enough to be lifted, bundled into the crate, and readied for what they clearly assumed would be a smooth flight back to Nigeria

British customs officers, however, noticed two glaring issues: the crate wasn't properly marked as a diplomatic bag, and it was about the same size as a person. When they opened it, they found Dikko slumped inside, along with an oxygen cylinder to keep him alive during transit.

The scandal that followed made headlines worldwide. Nigerian officials had assumed the diplomatic bag's immunity would protect them, but the sheer audacity of trying to smuggle a human being through Heathrow was too glaring to ignore. The operation failed spectacularly, leaving Dikko alive, unharmed, and probably more incredulous than anyone at the lengths his former government had gone to abduct him.

What I love the most about this story is that before his government was overthrown, Dikko's position was as the minister for transport.

A right tit

You're still thinking about the nipples aren't you?

OK.

Back to Budapest.

Having found a quiet corner of the office I phoned my wife. I asked her to do me a favour; Jump in the car, come to the office and grab Agi and my company debit card. Then I wanted her to take her to Hugo Boss on Vaci Utca and buy her a smart tailored suit for the wearing of tomorrow in our client meeting.

My wife - at the time - being my wife, agreed, on the condition that she could buy something for herself whilst she was there. I reluctantly agreed, making a note to square it away quietly with the Finance Director later on. Resorting to, if necessary, the fact that I knew he was playing spreadsheets with the delectable Andika behind Mrs Finance Director's back.

Next day. 08:55. I'm seated in a cosy corner of the Intercontinental Hotel's vestibule. Five-star luxury on the Pest side, looking out over the Danube, with Buda's hills brooding in the distance. I'd chosen a deep, overstuffed Chesterfield for my throne, because if you're going to deliver corporate updates before coffee kicks in, you might as well do it in comfort.

Surrounding the table sat three senior directors from the German car giant. Finance, HR, and, the top brass himself, the Regional Director for Central and Eastern Europe. I was mid-pour, filling his bone-white cup from the silver coffee pot I had ordered. The chair to my left remained empty. Reserved for Agi. She wasn't late. The meeting was set for 09:00 and I, being me, had arrived fifteen minutes early. The Germans, being German, were there when I arrived, having probably arrived at dawn to lay out their towels and secure our corner spot.

We were still in the pleasantries stage, skimming the surface of conversation before diving into KPIs and timelines. I had met the team before, either together or on their own, as we had been negotiating the terms of our relationship, and I genuinely like them all. They were sharp, comparatively humourless but honest, and not above a dry joke now and then.

Gunther, the regional boss, glanced over my shoulder toward the entrance which the hotel's finely liveried doormen were dutifully bookending.

"I think your colleague has arrived, Matt." He said.

I turned. Sure enough, Agi was making her entrance. One doorman held the door, for her the other followed her though with his gaze, his eyes locked upon her.

Even from a distance I could tell the outfit meant business. Brown flared trousers, razor-sharp tailoring, and a shimmering jacket cinched at the waist with a single button. She'd paired it with a lighter brown top that really accentuated her figure. Very sharp. Very stylish.

I returned to the coffee. "Right. Gunther, I can't remember if you take sugar or not, apologies."

He didn't reply. Still staring over my shoulder, eyes frozen.

"Gunther?" I said again.

His expression had shifted from the fixed smile of formal business to a blend of confusion and disbelief.

Something dropped in my stomach.

I spun round. Agi was on final approach. The trousers looked even better up close. The jacket was as elegant as it was daring. The problem was, beneath it, she wasn't wearing a light brown top. She was wearing *absolutely fucking nothing*.

With each stride, the puckered Areola majora of one breast would slide into view, vanish, then be replaced by its twin as she popped her nose out to sniff the air.

As Agi raised her hand to greet Gunther, the left one saw its chance and leapt free completely, Bursting from behind the curtains like an overenthusiastic pantomime Buttons.

Gunther's whole being was paralyzed.

"Matt?" he asked, voice tight, turning away from my colleague and squarely towards me.

I glanced at the others. The Finance Director appeared to be deeply engrossed in the mechanics of the lid of the coffee pot. Kati from HR, meanwhile, not unattractive herself, was eating up the view with a subtle smile and a glint in her eye.

Well, who would have thought it? I asked myself. You never can tell.

I stood, intercepted Agi, and leaned in, blocking the view.

"Agi. Back to the office. Now." I hissed.

Office? What the fuck was I thinking?

"No. Go home. Don't go near the office. I'll call you later."

Each word was said with a quiet force. I didn't want to give her room for any more misunderstandings.

"What? Matt, why?" she asked, her hand flying to her lips.

"Agi? You. Are. Fucking. Naked." I nodded towards the door. "Go."

She spun on her heel and made a sharp exit, jogging for the doors with one arm clutched across her chest like some flustered Victorian debutante. Oh, now she's bothered about modesty.

I turned back to the group and collapsed into my chair. There was no way to style this one out, no witty recovery, no clever pivot.

"I'm really sorry." I said, sincerely, but also unable to hide the trauma.

Gunther looked at me over the top of his reading glasses. His face was calm, composed.

"Do you have her replacement?" he asked, deadpan.

I held his gaze. Kati, cool as ever, lifted the coffee cup to her full lips.

"Do you have her number?" She asked.

Flat tired

This was going to be a fucking problem.

The thing is, I didn't win this particular German car giant client. That triumph belonged to the UK sales team. Their job was to chase the whales. Once harpooned, the client would be handed off to whichever country was best placed to service it. In this case, that meant Hungary. That meant me.

The UK salesforce was led by Gemma. No-nonsense, razor-sharp, and annoyingly good at her job. Her sidekick was a fresh-faced junior recruiter named Paul, barely out of nappies but already showing flashes of brilliance. I liked the lad. Still do. I even left him a glowing recommendation on LinkedIn in 2008, declaring him a sure bet for future greatness. I wasn't wrong. After leaving VCI, Paul went on to establish his very own firm which became a great success. I recently had the pleasure of collaborating with him on a project to, once again, open up a Central and Eastern European division. Whilst it was short-lived, I was there long enough to come to the realisation that even now, after all these years, he still works harder than the rest of his team combined.

But Gemma and me? We despised each other.

On paper, there was no real reason. She was a star recruiter, a genuine asset to the firm. She made the company a fortune, and by extension, made me richer every single day.

And yet, we fought like stray dogs over a bone.

At the time, I relished it. I was in my thirties, cocky, adrenaline-fuelled, every inch the swaggering alpha who charged into conflict while everyone else ducked for cover. I think that was it. She was exactly the same. We threatened each other, even if neither of us would ever admit it.

Live by the sword, and you're always a heartbeat from a blade between the ribs. In board meetings, I never missed a chance to twist the knife over one of her rare fuckups, and here I had offered her the opportunity on a silver platter to get a large one over on me. Technically, I outranked her, but in practice? She was too good to ignore. A rainmaker of her calibre demanded an audience, regardless of the org chart. Sales forgives all sins, and fuck, could she sell.

And now, here I was. Same crime scene, the other end of the same day. Nursing a large whisky in the Intercontinental's dimly lit lounge, running every possible *how-the-fuck-do-I-sort-this- out* scenario through my frazzled brain. I figured if there was such a thing as karmic balance, it might just favour a man reflecting on his fuckups in the very chair he committed them.

I loved the 'Interconti' as we called it.

As I said, it sits right on the edge of the Danube, all glass and steel and concrete. It didn't pander to Budapest's romantic past. Across the water are the Insta friendly baroque facades of Buda Castle and Fisherman's Bastion, while the InterContinental remains stark and modern

Locals still argued over whether it was an eyesore or a masterpiece. To some, it was a brutal interruption in the city's skyline. To others, it was honest. To me, it was nouveau riche, cash without class.

It was me.

It opened its doors in 1977, a product of Hungary's state-owned hotel industry under Communist rule. At a time when Hungary was carefully positioning itself as the 'Gateway to the West' this hotel was designed to impress foreign visitors while operating within the strict confines of a centrally planned economy.

Inside, the hotel aimed to offer a taste of Western luxury with marble floors, chandeliers, high ceilings, and a sprawling lobby designed to cater to diplomats, businesspeople, and foreign dignitaries who needed a secure and comfortable base while in Budapest. Though state-owned, the hotel was one of the few places where Western goods, from imported alcohol to luxury toiletries, were readily available, making it a magnet for those who lived behind the Iron Curtain but craved a glimpse of the capitalist world.

Its location was carefully chosen on the Buda side, overlooking the majestic Danube River and the Parliament building, offering views that combined Hungary's rich history with the promise of a changing future.

Over the years, the Intercontinental became more than just a hotel. It was a silent witness to Cold War intrigue, a meeting place for whispered negotiations and sometimes a staging ground for covert operations. Behind its polished facade, it hosted a steady parade of notable guests. Margaret Thatcher reportedly stayed here during her visits to Eastern Europe. Bill Clinton held meetings here during the 1990s.

2013. Freed by the BCC from the daily charade of getting up and pretending to work, I took the opportunity to fly to Budapest and sell the apartment on Zoltán Utca. The real estate market had surged, and the flat was now worth more than double the $50,000 I had paid for it only a few years earlier.

Back at the InterContinental, the bar was busier than usual. The Grand Prix had brought the city to life, and the hotel thrummed with red-clad Ferrari fans mingling with silver-clad Hamilton supporters. My own day had been a steady flow of apartment viewers, and I felt confident I would soon be rid of the place. Sitting with a drink in hand, I thought back to the contortions I had gone through to buy it in the first place.

At the time, I had, ahem, come into $50,000 in cash and needed a way to move it into my bank account without drawing the attention of the authorities. Converting it into Hungarian forints was simple enough. Budapest was full of exchange kiosks, and a couple of weeks wandering the city, changing a thousand dollars at a time, left me with a suitcase bulging with banknotes.

Getting it into the bank was the real problem, until I came upon an idea that seemed beautiful in its simplicity. My wife and I dressed for a night out and toured the four casinos in the city centre. At each roulette table she bet black, and I bet red. Apart from the two occasions when the wheel landed on green zero, the system was practically foolproof. By the end of the night we had almost the full amount of my original fortune, now neatly transformed into casino chips. We cashed them in, collected the crucial receipt, and walked away with the perfect safeguard should any official ever decide to ask awkward questions.

Our offer on the apartment had been accepted, and soon enough we were seated in the office of István, our lawyer, across the table from the seller and his attorney of choice. There had been no shortage of interest in the flat. It sat in the heart of downtown, overlooking the glistening Danube, and was the perfect size for one of the ever-growing army of students the city seemed to attract. Once the seller discovered I was a cash buyer, he had shaken my hand eagerly, and here we were, ready to sign.

The formalities were almost complete when I realised one crucial detail had been overlooked.

"So I suppose we just need Mr Varga's bank account details so I can make the transfer." I said, turning to István.

He translated my request, which was met with puzzled frowns from across the table. The seller muttered to his lawyer, who relayed it back to mine, who in turn began to explain to me.

"He said…" began István.

"Yes, I heard." I cut in. By this point, my Hungarian was more than adequate to follow the conversation.

"I *did* say I'm a cash buyer" I admitted. "The money is in my account. I don't need a mortgage."

My lawyer relayed this, and the seller reacted with outrage. He had assumed I would arrive with the same suitcase of notes I had spent weeks exchanging across the city, not to mention the long hours at roulette tables where my wife and I had slowly turned it into something the banks would accept. Instead, I was offering him something far less convenient: A taxable bank transfer.

We went back and forth before he grudgingly agreed. When the papers were signed and the keys finally passed across the table, I rose and shook his hand as he scowled.

"Dodgy bastard." I thought, slipping the keys into my pocket as I stepped out into the sunshine. The river shimmered in the distance, and just along the boulevard a casino's neon sign flickered invitingly. Perhaps I'd stop in, raise a glass, and put a little on red.

Big Swinging Dick

I set my empty glass down on the polished surface of the Intercontinental bar and let my fingers trace its rim. I looked up and caught the waitress's eye. I had come here to solve a puzzle, and I had learned that my sharpest thinking came alone in a crowd, a cold drink in hand, the buzz of strangers swirling around me. Their laughter, the snippets of conversation, the occasional clink of glass against glass all seemed to stimulate my thought processes.

Tonight, the puzzle in my head was deceptively simple: The name for my new company.

The firing had landed like a punch to the gut. Five years. Five years of loyalty of uprooting my family and moving three thousand miles across the planet, of nights spent alone in sterile hotel rooms while my children sat on the nanny's lap laughing at stories I should have been telling. And for what? Nothing.

I felt a betrayal so raw it burned through every part of me, deeper than any personal slight, deeper than a lover's infidelity could have cut. I had been closer to this job than to anyone else in my life, and they had torn it from me. Stripped me of my title, my colleagues, my office. Snatched the keys from my hand. I had built this empire brick by brick, through blood, sweat, and sleepless nights, and now they were trying to convince themselves it could exist without me.

The bar carried on around me - a symphony of noise, indifferent to my anger. Laughter, chatter, the hiss of pouring drinks.

The worst of it was not the loss, not even the humiliation. They had taken from me my sense of trust. Trust in people. Trust in the world I thought I understood. The obvious path - polish my CV, crawl back into the corporate machine - was gone. I couldn't face it, not now, not ever.

So I would carve my own path. I would build my own company, brick by brick, on my own terms. Nobody would ever strip away what I had created again, nobody could hurt me the way they had. And I would do it alone. My mind flicked back to the dozens of people I had once placed in the very positions that had thrown me down, and a pang of shame shot through me. I swore I would never do that again. Yes, my company would be big - it would dominate its sector - but it would always be just me. Just me.

Of course, the company I would set up had to be a recruitment company. That part was easy, that was all I had come to know. A few days before my flight to Hungary, I had been lounging by the pool, mentally ticking off potential sectors to focus on. IT? Absolutely not. I had always found IT roles maddening - CVs that seemed perfect would come back with a casual "no thanks". Property and construction? Booming in the Middle East, yes, but still too technical for my taste. Sales? Candidates too flaky. Finance? Clients too dry. Automotive? Aerospace? Agriculture?

Then it hit me, blindingly obvious. Recruitment. Of course. A sector I understood like the back of my hand. I had hired, managed, promoted, motivated, consoled, and yes, mercilessly fired hundreds of recruiters. It was everything I knew and everything I loved.

I took a long, celebratory pull on my ice-cold Carlsberg, watching my daughter launch herself from the edge of the pool onto a nearby lilo with alarming bravery. She landed, bounced, and waved triumphantly like she'd conquered Everest. A grin spread across my face. That, I thought, was exactly how I felt about my new venture: A daring leap into the unknown, slightly terrifying, and utterly exhilarating. I would be a Rec-to-Rec, a recruiter's recruiter. And, oh yes, I thought, eyes sparkling as I drained my pint, I knew exactly which company would be my first goldmine for wonderful candidates.

So there I was, surrounded by Hungarian petrolheads, wrestling with the most important decision of my new life: The name. I had already settled on my niche - senior recruiters. Higher salaries meant higher fees, and candidates with a decade or more under their belts had already proven they could do the job. My interviews would be a breeze, almost a formality.

The napkin in front of me remained stubbornly blank, the pen in my hand idle, waiting for a spark. I let my gaze drift over the crowd, their laughter fading into the background as I imagined the world I was about to enter. Marble-clad offices in Dubai, London, New York. Candidates in perfectly tailored suits, polished brogues catching the light, exuding confidence, competence - the cream of the crop, the Big Swinging Dicks.

I snatched the napkin closer and clicked my pen. The waitress placed a fresh glass before me, and, in that moment BSD Rec to Rec was born.

You might think naming a company isn't that deep, just a box to tick on the to-do list. Oh really? Take a look at some of these real-life corporations.

Analtech - A U. S. -based chromatography company.

Boring Company - Elon Musk's tunnelling venture.

Craps Technology - Stands for "Creative Reliable Advanced Programming Systems."

BJ Services - An oilfield services company.

While we're here, taking a brief, cheerful detour from the humdrum tale of my, let's be honest, fairly unremarkable life. Let's pause to examine some branding disasters that have baffled the world - and make you wonder how so many Marketing Directors managed to keep their jobs.

Pepsi's "Come Alive" in China - The marketing team at Pepsi probably thought they were onto a stroke of genius. Their iconic slogan, 'Come Alive with the Pepsi Generation,' was meant to evoke energy, youth, and vitality. Unfortunately, when translated into Chinese, it morphed into something more… literal: 'Pepsi brings your ancestors back from the grave.'

Coors' 'Turn It Loose' in Spanish-speaking countries - What could go wrong with a slogan meant to suggest relaxation and letting loose? Plenty, it turns out. 'Turn It Loose' was rendered in Spanish roughly as 'Suffer from diarrhoea.'

Ford Pinto - The Pinto is often cited in business schools for safety controversies, but its name carried its own headaches overseas. In Brazilian slang, 'pint'" is a crude term for male genitalia.

Mitsubishi Pajero - Mitsubishi didn't think twice about naming its SUV the 'Pajero.' In Spanish-speaking countries, however, Pajero simply translates as 'wanker.'

And my favourite, Gerber Baby Food in Africa - When Gerber expanded into some African markets, they used the same packaging as in the U.S, with a cute baby on the label. Unfortunately, in many regions, literacy rates were low, and some thought the label meant the contents were baby meat.

Big Bills for a Big Biller

The idea for BSD was born by the pool in Dubai, christened in the Intercontinental in Budapest, and finally, one quiet Sunday morning back in the sandpit, it came alive. I woke early, showered, dressed, walked across the landing into my study, switched on the desk lamp, opened my laptop, and sat down.

And just sat there.

For years, my mornings had followed the same ritual: A large coffee and a mountain of emails. Except this time there were no emails. No inbox, no outbox, not even an email address. No website, no logo, no terms of business. My LinkedIn profile was out of date. I had no database for CVs, and in any case, I had no CVs. That was fine, I told myself. Once I started advertising vacancies, they'd flood in. Except - I had no vacancies. No clients. No business.

The feeling reminded me of the day I first brought my newborn twins home from the hospital: The overwhelming certainty that life had shifted irreversibly, paired with the panicked realisation - Now what the fuck do we do?

I started with the logo. This was the age of Twitter and Skype, when minimalist branding was the mark of modernity. I couldn't very well sketch a literal BSD, so I chose instead a bold rendering of the letters against a deep blue, a quiet homage to the skies of my host country. Hours later, satisfied with my new corporate tattoo, I updated LinkedIn, bought a domain, set up an email, and wrote my auto signature.

And because I've always suspected nobody actually reads email disclaimers, I hid a line halfway through mine:

"This email and any attachments are intended only for the named recipient. If you are not the intended recipient, please notify us immediately, delete it from your system, and accept our apologies. (On the off chance you've read this far, let us know and we'll send you a bottle of wine.)"

Twelve years and tens of thousands of emails later, not a single person has claimed the wine.

From there, BSD caught a wave.

As far as I knew, there was only one other Rec-to-Rec in the Middle East, and he was frankly terrible. I'd used him once back when I was at Dream, and his candidate-led scattergun approach left me unimpressed.

There are two ways to build a recruitment desk: candidate-led or client-led. My way was client-first. I spoke to decision makers, understood exactly what kind of recruiter they wanted, then went to market and targeted only those people. Once I landed one, I'd present them to my client, the hire was made, and I got paid.

Recruiting recruiters is a strangely polarising business. One minute you're on the phone with someone who is sharp, charming, and utterly self-aware. They know the pressures you're under, because they live them every day themselves: The targets, the cold calls, the endless tightrope between client demands and candidate egos. Conversations with these people are a joy, a professional meeting of minds where you feel like you're actually talking the same language.

And then there's the other kind. The ones who remind you why recruiters have such a mixed reputation in the first place. Bitter, burnt-out, and itching for a fight. They don't see you as a potential partner in crime, just another bloody nuisance clogging up their diary. You become the lightning rod for every shitty week they've just had. Finally, here's someone they can unload on. Someone they can tell to fuck off - because let's be honest, they've had enough fuck offs themselves in the last five days to last a lifetime.

So, they give it back, with interest. And you hang up wondering if they actually hate you, or if they just hate the job, the industry, maybe even themselves.

Then there's a quirk of the Rec-to-Rec world you don't find anywhere else: The bosses of the very people you're approaching ringing or emailing to demand you stop poaching their staff. They discover it in all sorts of ways. Monitored inboxes and LinkedIn accounts are the usual suspects, though sometimes the candidate themselves gives the game away. A little ego massage, a casual *guess who's chasing me*, just to remind their boss they're in demand.

The irony of a recruiter telling another recruiter not to recruit is so thick you could spread it on toast.

My replies depend entirely on the manner of approach. If the message is polite - maybe with a nod to the absurdity of the situation, or a hint that the firm is going through a rough patch - I'll meet them halfway. Something along the lines of: Fair enough, I won't proactively target your people, but if they knock on my door, I'm throwing it wide open.

If, on the other hand, their tone is more blunt - demanding, aggressive, or dripping with entitlement - I don't hesitate. I match it, multiply it, and send it straight back.

Whilst the recruitment process may sound simple, it isn't easy. Good recruiters don't move lightly. They are usually sitting on a pile of deferred commission, owed but not yet paid, and walking away would mean leaving money on the table. You need a very good reason to tempt them out.

But those reasons exist. A toxic culture. A micromanaging boss. Meetings for meetings' sake. A friend having been fired. Shit coffee. Out of twenty or thirty calls, one or two recruiters would be in that exact position - and those were the ones I reeled in.

Candidate-led recruitment works differently. You set up shop, hang out a shiny sign, and wait. Eventually someone disgruntled knocks on your door, and you take their CV, stamp your logo on it, and fire it off to every consultancy email address you've scraped into your database.

Sometimes it works. But from the hiring manager's perspective, those CVs often bear little or no resemblance to the role they need filled. Even if by chance they like what they see, they know that same CV has landed with twenty other firms. Straight away, they have only a one-in-twenty chance of closing.

It's lazy, transactional, and devoid of real consultancy. It didn't take long before BSD became, by some distance, the dominant Rec-to-Rec in the region.

I ran the business for five years, pushing out from Dubai into Qatar, Bahrain, and Oman. True to my promise, I kept the headcount at one: Just me, a laptop, and a phone. Some years were good, others were great. I even rolled the dice on a radio advert - a reckless expense at the time - and could trace a couple of hundred grand's worth of business directly back to it. Proof, if ever it was needed, that fortune sometimes does favour the brave.

The money flowed in thick and fast. The problem was it flowed out just as quickly. The UAE is a wonderful place to live if you're on a fat salary with a corporate credit card footing the bill. But when you're the one paying, the glamour looks a little different. Many nights ended the same way: Me alone on the roof terrace, glass in hand, staring out over the neon sprawl and asking myself if I really needed to be here at all.

Because the truth is, recruitment doesn't require a gleaming skyline. It requires a phone, a laptop, and a willingness to grind. Our expansion meant I couldn't possibly be in every market we operated in, so why tether myself to any one of them? Why Dubai, when the work could just as easily be done from a farmhouse in the Dales?

The bills were relentless. The air conditioning alone was costing me two grand a month. The glass I was holding cost a tenner. And as the years rolled on, the business grew larger, the invoices fatter, the cheques I signed scarier. With every passing quarter, it became harder to justify the lifestyle. More and more, I found myself longing for something simpler, something more tangible: the crackle of a Yorkshire pub fire, a pint you didn't need a mortgage for, and the need to wear socks.

Scruffy ginger twat

It's Ed Sheeran's fault I finally made the decision to come home.

It's November 2017. The weather was simply perfect. Mid 20s, low humidity. Big John and I are propping up the bar in the clubhouse. Big John was big. Hence his nickname. A hulking Irishman with a beard blacker than the night and as thick as a mattress. He made a very healthy living as the man to go to when your car stopped working. Mechanic to the stars, or at least the expat community.

"Do you like concerts there, Matt?"

He was staring at his Guinness, whilst addressing me. Although he and I were good friends, Guinness was his first love.

"Erm, I'm not a massive concert goer really."

"No, me neither."

"I saw U2 in Marseille once, that was good. Bruce Springsteen at Bramall Lane, and my first concert was Marillion in Liverpool. Apart from that I don't think I've been to any others." I explained.

I had Big John saved in my phone as, 'Big John'. One time, after a particularly vigorous brunch, I found myself diving headlong out of a taxi outside of my villa whilst my children took a second from building mudpies in the garden to witness their dear father start the long post brunch crawl up the staircase to the sober sanctuary of his house - I must tell you much about the Dubai brunch scene - but first, Big John.

A couple of hours later, I haul myself out of bed, still in the shorts, shirt and Havaianas I brunched in, determined to have at least an hour with the twins before their bedtime. I won't describe the hour or so I spend searching for my phone, we all do it. You probably did it this week. But at 7pm I'm at my desktop, messaging my friends on Facebook asking them to call my phone. One duly did, and a good Samaritan by the name of Sonny answered, admitting, yes, he had found my phone in a taxi, and of course I could pick it up tomorrow.

My friends started chatting about my loss over our shared Whatsapp group. Big John announced to the chat that he had spoken to the temporary custodian of the telephone, and although he sounded like a geek and was most likely a homosexual type of person, he seemed trustworthy enough. Of course, Sonny, being in possession of my Samsung Galaxy, was also following the chat intently. He later told me, as we were to become firm friends and poker night buddies, that he was on the verge of telling us all to stick the phone up our respective arses, until he noticed the moniker of Big John and the profile picture akin to a very angry Bluto, and thought better of it.

"Ladies!" My friend Martin had bowled into the bar. I looked at the clock on the TV currently playing VH1. Ten past 4, Martin was 10 minutes late. We hadn't arranged anything specific but pick any random day at 4pm and if the 3 of us were not leaning on the polished mahogany in the clubhouse, then there had likely been a minor apocalypse somewhere.

Another big fellow, and a Northern Irish man, Martin and I were the closest of friends. We drank together, frequently, and ran a couple of side hustles, one of them involving peddling black market pork products to the bacon-starved British Diaspora in the Middle East.

I turned to greet him with a genuine smile. Martin was the most cheerful, entertaining and generous of characters you could hope to meet.

"D'ya like concerts there Martin?" Boomed big John as he held out his hand for Martin to grasp.

"Not really no." As he simultaneously shook John's outstretched hand with one arm and gave me a warm hug with the other, then to the barman, still clutching me to his bosom "The usual please, Boss."

The last request was redundant. Wilson, the Nigerian bartender already had the frozen pint glass underneath the Strongbow tap, dispensing the first of the 8 that Martin would have that evening before we all would exchange hugs and waddle back to our respective spouses.

"No, me neither." Admitted big John.

"Why do you ask?" This time me, resting my empty glass back on the bar and nodding to Wilson for another.

"Dis fella in MacGettigan's just gave me a pair of tickets." He said, inserting a meaty palm into his pillowcase of a jacket pocket and producing a couple of slips of paper."

I accepted them and studied the writing.

"Ed Sheeran." I said. "Fucking hell. VIP? Who gave you these?"

I don't know, some scruffy ginger twat I got talking to.

By coincidence, the thinking out loud video was playing on MTV.

"That's him." I said, indicating the large LCD screen hung above the bar.

John followed my gaze.

"Yep, dat's da fella." He said as he drew on his Guinness.

"No." I said "I mean that's Ed Sheeran.

"Oh really?" Said John. "Dat's da scruffy ginger twat." He drained his pint. "Nice fella."

John had been cheating on us in having a couple of pints elsewhere before we convened. The Scruffy Ginger Twat had asked him if the seat next to him was free, and on being told it was, he slid alongside John and asked him how his day was going. John surreptitiously nudged his laptop bag away from the SGT with his foot, you couldn't be too careful. I literally spat out my beer on hearing this part of the story.

"Tight bastard never even bought me a pint." Ruminated John, as he slipped the free VIP tickets back into his pocket.

Anyway, the Dubai brunching scene. Every Friday (for t'is not a workday) the Emirates' five-star hotels throw open the doors of their dining halls to hordes of thirsty air hostesses, recruitment consultants, financial advisors and a few unwitting tourists. For a small fee, ranging anywhere from the equivalent of £40 up to double that amount, the diners enjoy three or four hours of unlimited food and booze.

The closest comparison I can offer you is the day is akin to a ladies' day at one of the prominent racing events we host in our home country. Finely suited gentlemen with highly polished shoes and available debutantes offering a coquettish hint of decolletage, patiently yet excitedly awaiting opening time. Then, five or six o clock all across the city sees thousands upon thousands of inebriated expats as if extras in a zombie apocalypse movie. Ties wrapped around sweaty foreheads, high heels and knickers stuffed into Chanel handbags.

Every couple of years The Sun newspaper will carry a headline akin to 'Bonking Brit Banged up abroad' or 'Dazzling Diva Detained in Desert' Above a carefully selected Instagram picture of said female air hostess or recruitment consultant posing in front of the Burj Al Arab. There then follows the story of a previously flawless and law-abiding individual having been caught in the act of enjoying a knee trembler with an equally adorable lothario down one of Dubai's back alleys or on one of its darkening beaches, much to the chagrin of the local Fuzz.

Without exception, such liaisons have always taken place between six and seven pm, on a Friday, straight after a Brunch. Can't recommend them highly enough. The brunches that is.

Anyways. Ed Sheeran.

I wandered back to the villa that evening, the night air still warm against my skin. I'd just said loud, lingering goodbyes to Martin and Big John, two good souls, the kind who hug hard and laugh easily, and it left me feeling oddly hollow. The compound was buzzing, as usual. My wife and the kids were out again, swept up in one of the nightly villa parties that seemed to occur on a daily basis. The house, when I let myself in, greeted me with silence.

It was huge, quiet, and utterly empty.

I made my way to my office, a cool, shaded space at the back of the villa that still smelled faintly of wood polish and sun-warmed books. I sat at the heavy mahogany desk, the kind that demands respect even if you're only using it to check emails or pay a bill. Reaching to the side, I opened a cupboard that I probably used too often these days. Out came the bottle of whisky. Then a glass. I poured a generous slug, held it up to the light like some kind of half-hearted ceremony, then decided generous wasn't going to cut it tonight. I topped it off until it was virtually magnanimous.

I held it aloft in a silent toast to my dad. He would have understood. Probably wouldn't have said much, but he would have understood. Then I drank half of it in one long pull.

I was in a strange mood, one of those moods that creeps in behind you on padded feet when the noise stops and you find yourself alone with the facts. I had this nagging sensation, like I was living the same day on a loop: work, pub, come home to an echo. Repeat. I adored my kids, truly, but during the week I only saw them when they were asleep or in passing. Their mother? If I'm honest, I felt little more than politeness. The more parties she threw herself into, the less I had to pretend otherwise.

The glass was empty. I filled it again. The bottle hit the bottom of the waste basket with a hollow clink. That sound felt familiar too.

I turned to my laptop, clicked the YouTube icon out of habit more than thought. Music was what I needed, but not the kind that lifts you. It was far too late in the evening, and too far into the whisky, for anything triumphant. What my melancholy needed was company. Something that understood the mood I was in without asking questions.

YouTube had Ed Sheeran waiting for me. Of course it did.

The laptop was wired into the villa's wireless speaker system. A ridiculous luxury, but one I appreciated in that moment. I sank into the old armchair in the corner of the study just as the crisp, aching guitar riff that opens Castle on the Hill sliced cleanly through the silence.

It suited the moment perfectly: Wistful, familiar, and just a little bit sad.

The first chords echoed through the office, crisp and familiar, and I felt something shift in my chest. Suddenly I wasn't in a villa surrounded by expensive silence. I was back in South Yorkshire, 18 again, with an old banger in the drive and rain on the windows, and I missed it.

Ed started singing, and the words hit harder than I expected.

"I found my heart and broke it here…"

I sank deeper into the chair. The whisky burned slightly less this time, or maybe I was just numb to it now. The line wasn't just a lyric; it was a mirror. I couldn't even remember the last time I felt my heart doing anything other than beating out of duty. Breaking, at least, would mean it still cared.

I thought of my dad again. I think Ed's songs do that to people, drag up the ghosts, not just of people you've lost, but of who you used to be. Dad would've told me to get some sleep, or to take a walk, or to stop being so bloody dramatic. But he'd have known what I meant.

"Made friends and lost them through the years…"

There they were, faces I hadn't seen in decades. Nick, who always brought his guitar to the park. Claire, who smoked Rothmans cigarettes and had a laugh that stayed in your head for days. My mates from sixth form, all of us sure we'd stay close forever. But forever doesn't account for jobs, different cities, partners, kids.

I hadn't spoken to most of them in years. Some I hadn't thought about until this very moment. That made me feel worse, somehow. Like I'd abandoned not just people, but whole versions of myself.

The track moved into that verse, the one about friends scattered, damaged, surviving in their own small ways. One with kids but living alone. One's brother overdosed. Each line felt like another little tug on something painful and frayed inside me.

I took another sip and held it in my mouth longer this time.

How had I ended up here, of all places? In a sun-drenched villa on the other side of the world, with children I loved but barely saw awake, a marriage I had long since stopped pretending to care about, and a social life that depended entirely on a bunch of friends who listed our clubhouse as next of kin?

"Driving at 90 down those country lanes. . ."

The lyric hung in the air as I turned toward the window, where another choking orange desert sandstorm was gathering on the horizon. In my mind, I was back on the winding, sweet-smelling and oh-so-green roads of Yorkshire.

My old Mini couldn't have hit 90 even if it had been pushed off a cliff, but that didn't matter. In that moment, I would have traded every supercar in my garage for one more chance to be eighteen again, windows down, music on, and going nowhere but forwards.

Homesickness isn't always about geography. Sometimes it's about time. About missing the person you used to be when the world felt more wondrous and the future full of possibilities.

The song was winding down now, the final lines washing over the office like low tide.

"I'm on my way…"

I wasn't, though. I wasn't on my way anywhere.

I stared at the bottom of my glass for a long time before setting it down on the armrest. The room was still. That strange mix of peace and ache that only comes late at night, with good whisky and fond memories.

I considered playing something else, maybe something lighter. But that felt dishonest. The truth was, for the first time in a long while, I wanted to feel it. The ache, the emptiness, the years slipping away like desert sand through my fist. I didn't want to drown it out or distract myself. I wanted to sit with it, accept it, confront it, and come to terms with it. Just for a little longer.

And I poured one more drink. And I decided there and then. I'm going home.

Epilogue

When do you call time on the telling of a life? I'm still here, inconveniently alive, and things happened just yesterday that you and I won't get to discuss. Things will likely happen tomorrow too. Could be trivial, could be sublime.

What if, the moment I close this laptop, King Charles knocks on the door scratching his bollocks and asking to borrow a fiver for a scratchcard?

You'll never know.

Right now, we're still back in 2017. I'm following my family up the steps of an Emirates A380, bound for Manchester. It's the largest passenger aircraft ever built – obviously - Four million individual parts went into its making. Each one, concerningly, sourced from the lowest bidder. That fact alone gave me pause as I boarded.

Much has happened since that day. So much, in fact, that I've lost track of who I was when we left. We never saw the sunlight of Dubai again. Never really looked back. But a story, like a journey, must disembark somewhere.

Has anyone ever written their memoir to the very end? Typed out their final sentence with their final breath? You'd have to be a meticulous bore to pull that off. Technically accurate, yes, but tragically unreadable. You never get to publish your book. Or hold it. Or autograph the straining T-shirt of a divorced mum or go on Loose Women.

Every memoir, by its very nature, ends prematurely. Just like we do. We bow out mid-paragraph, with unfinished plans, unspent savings and half-raised children, left to navigate this journey alone and write their own book.

So, let's leave it here.